Me and Mine

Me and Mine

The Triumph of the
New Individualism?

John Rentoul

with Jane Ratford

UNWIN

HYMAN

LONDON SYDNEY WELLINGTON

First published in Great Britain by Unwin Hyman Limited, 1989

UNWIN HYMAN LIMITED
15–17 Broadwick Street, London, W1V 1FP

Allen & Unwin Australia Pty Ltd
8 Napier Street, North Sydney, NSW 2060, Australia

Allen & Unwin New Zealand Pty Ltd
with the Port Nicholson Press
Compusales Building, 75 Ghunzer Street
Wellington, New Zealand

British Library Cataloguing in Publication Data

Rentoul, John
   Me and Mine: The triumph of the new
   individualism?
1. Great Britain. Political ideologies.
Individualism
I. Title
320.5'12'0941
ISBN 0-04-440193-0

Typeset in 10 on 12 point Sabon
and printed in Great Britain by
Billing and Sons Ltd
London and Worcester

By the same author

The Rich Get Richer

Contents

Acknowledgements

This book would not have been possible without a generous grant from the Kathleen Blundell Trust. I am very grateful to its assessors, Richard Hoggart, Michael Holroyd, Anne Smith and Philip Ziegler, and to Mark le Fanu, General Secretary of the Society of Authors, which administers it.

The book is a joint project with Jane Ratford, who carried out most of the interviews with former Labour voters on which the analysis is based. Without her exceptional ability to draw people out it would have been one boring opinion poll after another. She also did much of the early research.

Many thanks to John Lloyd and Stuart Weir, editors of the *New Statesman*, for allowing me time off to work on the book, and to all my colleagues at what is now *New Statesman and Society* for their support. Thanks also to: Deborah Mattinson; Harriett Gilbert: Anne McDermid; Roger Jowell and Sharon Witherspoon at Social and Community Planning Research for advice and data from the British Social Attitudes surveys; John Curtice; Bob Wybrow and Jane Richards at Gallup; Bob Worcester, Brian Gosschalk and Robin Taylor at MORI.

Introduction

When the Conservatives won their third consecutive election victory in 1987, it seemed to herald the triumph of individualism. All commentators and politicians agreed that the Thatcher Revolution had transformed the values of the British people; that people were more selfish; that Margaret Thatcher had pursued the politics of greed, and a greedier nation had voted for her. The message received from the working class of the South and East was: 'I'm all right, Jack.' Private was good, public was inefficient and second rate. Private houses, private health care, private education and privatised share issues were better than their public counterparts. What I have is mine. The 1980s were, it seemed, the Me and Mine Decade.

Mrs Thatcher, the greatest national leader since Elizabeth I according to the *Sunday Telegraph*, had partly brought about this dramatic change of heart in the British people, and partly reflected it. 'I sort of regard myself as a very normal, ordinary person with all the right, instinctive antennae,' she said in 1980 (*The Sunday Times*, 3 August 1980). She claims to have reinforced traditional moral values and restored a sense of responsibility, hence raising productivity and turning round the perception of Britain abroad.

The triumphalists of Tory individualism claim that more people now recognise that looking after their own economic interests is the best way of looking after everybody's interests, as Adam Smith once said. (Adam Smith said other things, too, such as: 'All for ourselves and nothing for other people seems, in every age of the world, to have been the vile maxim of the masters of mankind' – *Wealth of Nations*, p. 512. But pass over that for a moment.) The moral transformation of the British people has produced more demanding consumers, more responsible citizens, a nation of enterprising spirits standing on their own two feet.

Critics call it selfishness. Defenders call it self-reliance. More neutrally, it is called individualism, and everyone seems to think

xi

there is more of it. The post-war consensus has broken up, and the British, particularly the prosperous working class but also the liberal middle class, have become more likely in the 1980s to see their interests as being served by their own endeavours in the market than by collective action, whether by trade unions or the state.

This book started off as an analysis of why the Conservatives were winning the argument in every policy area with the notion that private is better than public. 'Opting out' was the dominant theme in housing, education, trade union law and even health care. 'Individualism versus collectivism' seemed to be the way to analyse the 1987 election campaign and its triumphalist aftermath. There were two other very simple explanations for Mrs Thatcher's third victory – the divided opposition and the steady rise in living standards for the majority. But they, too, seemed to be connected to the triumph of individualism. Part of the appeal of the Liberal–SDP Alliance appeared to be its diluted individualist programme: individualism with a collectivist conscience. And growing prosperity meant that more people could afford to express their individualist desires and opt out of public services.

The Labour Party had impressed everyone with its election campaign, but it seemed that nowadays people were more interested in cash than compassion.

Yet opinion polls and surveys, such as the British Social Attitudes surveys, suggest that people have actually become more left wing in their basic values since the annual surveys began in 1983. And the consistent questions that the Gallup organisation had asked on issues such as the NHS, trade unions, the welfare state and the role of government generally showed that public opinion either had not changed or had become more 'collectivist' since 1979.

The triumph of collectivism

There are three voices which have tried to make themselves heard above the hubbub of Me and Mine triumphalism.

John Curtice, a lecturer in politics at the University of Liverpool, detected the shift to the left in people's values since the 1983 General Election in his analysis of the British Social Attitudes series. After the 1987 election he stuck to his guns, saying that Social Attitudes research showed that the government had won despite being out of touch with people's values because of the economic boom and the electorate's lack of confidence in the Labour Party's ability to manage the economy.

Secondly, John MacInnes, an industrial relations expert at Glasgow University, has published a book called *Thatcherism at Work* which explodes the myth that the Thatcher government has changed hearts and minds in the workplace. The assumptions governing British industrial relations, he says, have *always* been highly individualistic. Labour governments tried through incomes policies to make wage negotiators take the wider collective interests of society into account; the Conservatives have simply abandoned the unemployed and the low-paid to market forces that were loaded so heavily against them. There is no 'new realism' on the shopfloor, just new mass unemployment outside it.

And thirdly, David Marquand, a sort of guru to the non-Owenite wing of the Social Democratic Party before its merger with the Liberals, has published his discussion of Thatcherism, *The Unprincipled Society*. In it he suggests that the problems of Britain's relative social and economic decline over the past century were caused by too little collectivism, not too much, and traces the historical origins of deeply entrenched individualistic attitudes.

These three authors challenge the idea that there has been a triumph of individualism in different ways and in different contexts. John Curtice goes so far as to claim that the country has been moving away from Thatcherite values under the very government that sought to ensure their permanent ascendancy. MacInnes and Marquand assert instead that Britain has always been more 'Thatcherite' than had been thought, and urgently needs to be less so. But all three assert that there is an alternative to the triumphalist interpretation of recent British history.

So there are two contrary views of what has happened in contemporary Britain. One, that prevailing attitudes and values have changed, becoming more individualistic and more accepting of free-market ideas; the other that, in general, they haven't, that people are just as collectivist as they have always been (which may not have been as much as was once taken for granted), if not actually more so. The values of cooperation and altruism are not to the fore in the political arena for obvious reasons:

the government doesn't believe in them and can win elections without endorsing them.

It may seem a straightforward matter to arbitrate between these two competing interpretations. But first the triumph of individualism has to be defined more accurately, because when it is examined more closely it changes shape. The claims of the triumphalists are riddled with contradictions, assertions which don't follow from premises, confusions between what people think and what politicians and intellectuals argue about, and simplifications of and condescensions towards the motivations of 'ordinary' people.

Chapter 1, The 'Thatcher Revolution', tries to untangle the knots that get in the way of clear thinking, to stand back and look at the millions of words that have been written and delivered in attempted explanation of 'Thatcherism' and, in particular, the result of the 1987 General Election. Once what is actually at stake is isolated, the rival claims can be tested against the attitudes and values of real people in the following chapters. The evidence of opinion surveys and in-depth interviews is that there is a big gap between what people think and what the government wants them to think.

There are two kinds of evidence for most things: the scientific and the anecdotal. Usually scientific evidence is the more reliable. But this investigation deals with the intangible – people's attitudes and values – and so does not rely solely on political scientists and their opinion polls. The core of this book is a range of interviews with mostly working-class people who used to vote Labour – the alleged new individualists. This is anecdotal evidence. But in-depth interviewing can tell us much more about the *quality* of people's attitudes and values than opinion polling.

The opinion poll evidence destroys the notion that the British people have become more selfish (or self-reliant). The in-depth interviews help to explain why not, and why we might have thought they had.

The concluding chapter looks at what happens when the conventional wisdom that the British have become more individualistic in the 1980s is overturned. The fact that the Thatcher governments have *not* achieved the triumph of individualism has profound implications for British politics into the 1990s. It sheds light on the old, gloomy question, 'must Labour lose?' That question dominated British politics in the early 1960s, after the last time Labour lost a third election in a row, in 1959. Some of the parallels with 1987 are striking, especially the similar panic on the Left over the affluent working class, which was widely thought to be infected with Tory individualism. But things are different now, and another important question which needs to be answered is: 'Will the centre hold?' The Liberal Party in 1959 polled a mere 6 per cent of the vote amid talk of a breakthrough. In 1987 the Liberal–SDP Alliance won 23 per cent and was counted a failure. Since then the merged Social and Liberal Democrats have struggled to establish an identity.

The fact that the values of cooperation and collective welfare are just as strong as, if not not stronger than, they were has important consequences, too, for the Conservative Party and the succession to Margaret Thatcher. If the Tories can win three elections in a row while espousing unpopular values, think what they could do (against a reviving Labour Party for instance) if they espoused popular ones. Meanwhile, the Labour Party and the Democrats are both trying to define what they believe in and to review their policies. Deputy Labour leader Roy Hattersley's contribution has been to emphasise individual liberty as the goal of democratic socialism, in part as a direct response to Mrs Thatcher's individualist appeal; but the foundations of Labour's philosophy remain imbued with Neil Kinnock's collectivist instincts. A philosophy which, apart from a different view of trade unions, does not differ significantly from that of the centre party. The concluding chapter argues that the opposition parties, in their attempts to match Mrs Thatcher and to differentiate themselves from each other, should not confuse individualism with selfishness: it is the non-Conservatives who have a better claim to be the true individualists, in the sense of believing in genuine independence for more of the people.

Me and Mine

1

The 'Thatcher Revolution'

If there is an individualism that has triumphed, it should be possible to set out what it might consist of, and then to see if it has. The triumphalists claim that there has been a change in the attitudes and values of the British electorate in the 1980s, particularly among the prosperous working class but also among acronymously upwardly mobile 'yuppies'. These new individualists are seen as more materialistic and less guilty about being selfish. Either they don't care about those less fortunate than themselves, or they believe that by attending to their own wealth creation, the general prosperity will soon enough seep through to the less fortunate.

More specifically, the new individualists are more likely to prefer private provision of services to public provision of education, housing and health care. And not just for themselves, but for everyone else too, in order to reduce the cost of providing public (or, more pejoratively, 'state') services so that they may in turn enjoy the benefits of tax cuts. Individualists are sceptical of, if not actually hostile to, institutions purporting to represent a collective interest, paramount among them the state, including local government, but also trade unions and, much less emphasised, big corporations.

The historical moments of the triumph of individualism are 1979 and 1987: the first was the decisive break with the failed postwar (collectivist) consensus, the second a triumphal endorsement of the 'Thatcher Revolution'. This was the nearly unanimous theme of political commentators for a year after the 1987 General Election – even if they disagreed about what the opposition parties should do about it.

The fullest example of the genre is Peter Jenkins' book, published at the end of 1987, called *Mrs Thatcher's Revolution: The Ending of the Socialist Era*.[1] Mrs Thatcher had, he asserted, 'presided over

1

a considerable, although far from complete, change in attitudes. [A new] "common ground" has been established. Its assumptions are individualistic rather than collectivist, preferring private to state ownership, putting the rights of the member before the interests of the trade union, and sound money above the priming of the economy' (p. 375).

Of course, the idea of a Thatcher Revolution wasn't invented in 1987; a dramatic change in public opinion was thought to have occurred in or before 1979, following the crisis of the post-war consensus in the mid-1970s, the origins of which some commentators located even earlier.

Jenkins argues that 'Margaret Thatcher was as much a consequence as a cause of the collapse of the *ancien regime*, a product of the ending of the socialist era. She was Britain's first post-socialist prime minister' (p. 378).

Originally, it was the New Right wing of the Tory Party which alleged that British government for the whole of the post-war period until 1979 was 'socialist' in character. But now centrists like Jenkins and Tory moderates like Kenneth Baker have adopted the same version of the triumph of individualism, which is that it was the inevitable response to the triumph of socialism in 1945, because socialist collectivism was bound to collapse under the weight of its contradictions.

In a speech to the Bow Group, on 27 April 1988, Baker, then the man most likely to succeed Margaret Thatcher, took as his theme 'the failure of collectivism and the emergence of the new individualism'. The old collectivism, he said, was typified by Clement Attlee and the new individualism by Margaret Thatcher. Effectively, Attlee governed Britain from 1945 until 1979, 'the break with collectivism'. The Attlee Labour government of 1945 inherited a state mobilised for total war, and so 'all the powers of the state, all the machinery to ration and direct resources, were harnessed for the purpose of building the New Jerusalem. The ethos of war time was to be imposed during peacetime. The individual's interests were to be subsumed into the collective good.'

The thirteen years of Conservative government, 1951 to 1964, 'redecorated rather than rebuilt' the socialist architecture. 'Indeed for the period from 1950 to 1970 it could be said we were all collectivists then.' Thus Baker dismissed two decades of British history, and a period of Conservative rule four years longer (at the time he spoke) than the one of which he was part, as a long and mistaken socialist administration.

Such prolonged error was bound to lead to trouble. Indeed, with the benefit of a little hindsight, New Right writers James Buchanan and Richard Wagner claimed to detect in 1960s Britain 'a generalised erosion in public and private manners, increasingly liberalised attitudes towards sexual activities, a declining vitality of the Puritan work ethic, deterioration in product quality, explosion of the welfare rolls [and] widespread corruption in both the private and the governmental sector' (*Democracy in Deficit: The Political Legacy of Lord Keynes*, pp. 64–5). By the time their book was published in 1977, the inevitable crisis had occurred, with the Labour government unable to hold the collectivist state together by borrowing money.

A reaction was bound to follow, and it was chronicled by younger New Righters David Graham and Peter Clarke in a Channel 4 series and book in 1986, *The New Enlightenment*, which 'explored the liberal revival all over the world'. For Graham at least, the Thatcher Revolution was also a personal political odyssey from left to right across the political spectrum. Like so many of Damascus's commuters, he identifies a personal transformation with one in the world at large. 'My world changed,' he wrote. 'One by one, assumptions were abandoned, friends lost and others gained. [But] our excitement has never wavered. We have never doubted, not for a minute, that we are looking at the greatest political shift of our century' (*The New Enlightenment*, p. xii). One hundred years ago, George Bernard Shaw was sceptical of 'the gushing enthusiasts who mistake their own emotions for public movements'; today, even the economic simplicities of the gushing enthusiasts are the same as they were in 1892.[2]

Graham and Clarke's argument is that the philosophy of the post-war consensus – Beveridge's welfare state, nationalisation and full employment – contained the seeds of its own destruction. 'A policy inspired by this philosophy will tend to set up institutions that help the middle class more than the working class, and give a high standard of service to no one very much.' As if in proof, they cite the case of William Benton, a 65-year-old former ship worker, who had to wait two years for the NHS to operate on him to seal a wound caused by an operating error when his gall bladder was removed. They say: 'We do not believe it is particularly unusual.' Hence: 'The truth is that the National Health Service is in poor shape.' And the cause: the fact that NHS is a public monopoly, not subject to market pricing.

A welfare state that creates national monopolies to provide services to its people will create institutions that give a poor and declining service to the public, favouring the strong against the weak. It will destroy the very habits and institutions that raise the poor from poverty and make all people productive and free.

Far from being an 'exploration' of the liberal revival, however, *The New Enlightenment* is simply an argument for it. I shall argue against it in later chapters, but not until the evidence has been examined.

Other explanations of the alleged collapse of collectivism are as imprecise as *The New Enlightenment*'s. According to Samuel Beer (*Britain Against Itself*, 1983), the post-war consensus started to break down in the mid-1960s, with the student revolts of 1968 as the key date in the changing of people's attitudes: 'the collapse of deference'. Collectivism – 'that thrust of policy, emerging in this century, toward control over the economic and social order as a whole' – began to break down because of its contradictions: the 'three scrambles', the pay scramble, benefits scramble and subsidy scramble, that Beer says couldn't go on indefinitely.[3]

This I call the 'hippy theory' of individualism: that the breakdown of the corporate state began with the 'permissive' revolution in national morality in the late 1960s, which made the pursuit of individual desires a more legitimate goal in life, weakening responsibilities to groups, the wider family (beyond the four-person nucleus) and the state. According to the hippy theorists, this attitude has now trickled through even to people who disapprove of permissive personal morality. The 'basic notion' of 1968, according to Peter Jenkins in *The Independent*, was 'inimical to collectivism, [it was] that freedom consisted in individual control over life and experience. Thatcherite populism was another aspect of the backlash against corporatism and statism' (5 January 1988).

This kind of explanation is not favoured by Conservatives. For them, 1979 has more resonance than 1968. Kenneth Baker gave four reasons why collectivism failed in his Bow Group speech. The first was that 'collectivism was not compatible with the basically individual instincts of the British people'. This is also how Margaret Thatcher interprets 1979: 'I really think that [my government] was the turn of the tide. We were slipping so fast into a socialist state, that the individual mattered less and the collective more. That's not right for the British character' (*The Times*, 28 March 1986). But, apart from not being right for the British character, which has presumably been true since at least 1066, how did the triumph of individualism come about?

Baker's second explanation was that 'collectivism depended on high taxation'. (This, too, is a little unconvincing: taxes are always 'too high', and though they may have risen during the post-war period the British level was average by international standards.) The third was that 'collectivism failed to deliver an internationally competitive economy. There seemed to be no penalties for failure and no rewards for success.' Fourth, 'collectivism was revealed to be morally inadequate'. As an analysis of historical causation this is dubious, but as a frontal assault on the Kinnockite monopoly of compassion it makes a lot of sense for 1990s Toryism, and for Baker's claim to the Thatcherite inheritance. Baker argued that collectivism 'failed to take into account individual human aspirations. The individual was absolved of responsibility for caring because this was now to be undertaken by the state. The traditional role of the family was weakened as an alternative network of dependency based on the state increasingly took its place.'

The only mechanism that Baker suggests could have achieved the Thatcher Revolution is rational thought. During the 1970s the British people considered Mr Baker's Four Failures and came to a conclusion by a process of logical deduction.

By 1979 it was clear that Britain was in an intellectual cul de sac so long as it persisted in having its vision restricted by the architecture of collectivism. The time had come to dismantle it, and the instrument was to be Margaret Thatcher's government of 1979. The Prime Minister's instinct was to return to individual aspiration and to encourage individuals to provide for themselves. From that would follow organically the growth of the national good. This view was almost revolutionary. It represented the liberation of individualism.

Either that, or the individualist values were always there, lying dormant, and were at last been given political expression by an inspired leader.

However, once the voters had come to their senses (after thirty years wandering, lost, on the fruitless plains of collectivism), Kenneth Baker's thesis becomes slightly more convincing. The mechanisms by which the Thatcher Revolution was allegedly *secured* – after 1979 – are more credible than the mechanism by which it was *achieved* in the first place.

One mechanism is what I call the Thatcher theory of individualism: that Mrs Thatcher, by sheer force of personality, strength of conviction or deep mystical communion with 'the British character', converted people through political evangelism; or, less dramatically, that the Conservative government and Prime Minister articulated and reinforced political values through propaganda and image management.

The other mechanism is the bull market theory: that the consecutive years of rising prosperity (for two-thirds or three-quarters of the population) since 1982 have been delivered by what Baker called the 'almost-revolutionary' programme: control of inflation, de-control of the exchange rate, tax cuts, curbing the trade unions, council house sales, privatisation. These policies enabled more and more people to discover that unrestrained individualism was right for their character.

As Mrs Thatcher put it: 'Economics are the method; the object is to change the soul' (*Sunday Times*, 3 May 1981). The new soul of the British people is the product of her will. 'I came to office with one deliberate intent. To change Britain from a dependent to a self-reliant society – from a give-it-to-me to a do-it-yourself nation; to a get-up-and-go instead of a sit-back-and-wait-for-it Britain' (*The Times*, 9 February 1984).

It is a goal that Mrs Thatcher claims to have achieved. This overlooks the fact that at least part of the triumph of individualism is supposed to have been a spontaneous change in public attitudes and values *before* Mrs Thatcher came to power; it also glosses over the very different character of her two administrations. In her first term, Mrs Thatcher's nationalism often seemed rather more important than her individualism. Many analysts attributed her success in the 1983 election to the Falklands war the year before, which seemed to overcome the effects of the deep recession of 1980–1 and the rise in unemployment from 1.3 to 3 million.

Indeed, in Mrs Thatcher's first term the rise of individualism was sometimes attributed to another cause altogether, what I call the armadillo theory: that under conditions of national and international uncertainty it is 'a sound pragmatic strategy for people to put their resources of time, energy and skill into making their domestic world more secure. At least in that sphere they have some control', as two sociologists put it in one 1981 study.[4] This might be called the 'psychotic' explanation of individualism. It is related to the idea that the growth in the Do-It-Yourself market represents an increasing tendency to focus on the home as the source of satisfaction rather than, say, work or social life.

But, by the time of the 1983 election, living standards for most of those in work had been rising strongly for eighteen months. The main condition for Mrs Thatcher's 144-seat landslide was the division of the opposition vote into two almost equal halves, but the economy was the main positive reason for voting Conservative, rather than the Falklands Effect, according to a detailed assessment by the University of Essex.[5]

The 1987 General Election

By 1987, real living standards for most people had been rising for five years, and the election appeared finally to confirm the unpopularity of even well-packaged collectivism in the shape of the Kinnock Labour Party.

The opposition accused the Conservative government of buying votes: of engineering prosperity for the 'haves' in the South and East and using it to turn working people away from their old collective values, now confined to the 'have nots' in the ghettoes of the inner cities and the occupied territories of the North and West. While Mrs Thatcher stood accused of encouraging 'greed and grab' (by David Steel), the opposition parties wrung their hands in righteous despair at the venality of their erstwhile supporters – at the same time as gingerly repackaging their image and policies in order to appeal to these new individualists.

Four weeks after the 1987 election Labour Party leader Neil Kinnock said: 'With the dispersal of the population, the experience of being part of a collective is not as strong as it used to be. Our initial approach has got to be from the party to the individual. They have got to be told that socialism is the answer because it looks after the individual' (*New Statesman*, 10 July 1987). He needed this fundamental shift towards individualism among the electorate in order to explain Labour's poor showing, because the quality of Labour's campaign was not available as an excuse as it had been in 1983.

Full-blooded revisionism along these lines could have gained momentum. Doug Jones, who was economic adviser to Labour's deputy leader Roy Hattersley, wrote in *The Guardian* of 'Mrs Thatcher's ownership revolution', and the need for Labour to 'emphasise its policies for the regulation of financial services in order to protect the new army of small savers and shareholders' (3 July 1987). But then party campaign manager Bryan Gould got it in the neck for being (erroneously) reported as saying that Labour should positively encourage people to buy shares.

He was the first victim of a defensive rearguard action fought not by people who denied that selfishness and greed had triumphed but by a wide range of commentators from pop stars to bishops who accepted that they had, and who thought this was to be deplored and attacked, rather than given in to and accommodated.

The rearguardists' criticisms of the Me and Mine decade built up to a crescendo after Nigel Lawson's 1988 Budget, which gave away some £2,000 million to the richest one-twentieth of the population. Andrew Phillips, a City solicitor giving the 1988 Hibbert Lecture was positively apocalyptic: 'In the post-Christian Eighties, the intensity and universality of materialist influences are today unprecedented, and close to creating a cultural melt-down throughout the developed world.'[6]

Kenneth Baker took these criticisms head on in his Bow Group speech: 'Our critics argue that our society is obsessed with material acquisition, that selfishness has replaced concern for others, and that private greed prevails over public need. Even the word "wicked" has been bandied about by a bishop,' said Baker candidly.

[But] I do not think there is any reason to apologise for the increased scope we have given for what might be called acquisitive individualism. Those who already have much should not look down on the desire to own of those who do not. The fact is that for millions of people the dispersal of economic power and wealth has brought greater individual freedom. It has meant economic and political independence. Fewer people are now beholden to the state or to the local council. I do not accept that this drive for self improvement is selfish.

The assertion that wealth and power has been dispersed will be contested in later chapters, but no doubts occlude Baker's confident final claim: 'The new individualism has been established.'

The *Financial Times* commented on the Budget:

> The rewriting of the income tax code is only part of a much wider social transformation. Mrs Thatcher and her ministers are successfully remoulding British attitudes. Evangelical speeches about enterprise and the magic of the market, which many would have taken about as seriously as water divining in the 1960s, are today received in solemn silence. Nobody jokes about the big E (for enterprise) that adorns the wall of Lord Young's Trade and Industry Department. We are all being re-programmed as enthusiastic free-marketeers. (Michael Prowse, 19 March 1988)

The same basic idea was put in an equally extravagant but more partisan way by Bruce Anderson in the *Sunday Telegraph* on 17 April 1988:

> Economic recovery has been accompanied by social transformation. In particular, the spread of ownership, especially home ownership, has turned the 'property-owning democracy' from a slogan into a reality. This is having profound political effects. One of Shaw's characters wanted to abolish the British working class and replace them with sensible persons: Mrs Thatcher has succeeded in doing just that. All the continuity, much of the richness, and many of the eccentricities of British history are explained by the fact that we never had a bourgeois revolution. But we are having one now – or at least a petit-bourgeois revolution.

Extravagant or smug, right wing or left wing, the unanimity is remarkable. 'We hold these truths to be self evident: that there has been a transformation in the attitudes and values of the British people; collectivism is dead, long live individualism.' It is all very interesting. But is it true?

The counter-revolution

The first signs that the triumph of Tory individualism was less complete than it seemed came from the Tory Party itself. Less than a year after the alleged triumph of individualism at the 1987 General Election, some Conservatives were infected by doubts, not about the reality of that triumph but about the wisdom of going too far. Already the government's individualist rhetoric had been qualified by Chancellor Nigel Lawson's U-turn on public spending in 1986 and the pre-election propaganda emphasis on the Conservatives as the high-spending party, especially on the National Health Service but also on social security. But in the spring of 1988, one Cabinet minister after another started to stress the duty of the new rich to give to charity, culminating in Margaret Thatcher's 'Sermon on the Mound', her address to the Assembly of the Church of Scotland, in Edinburgh, in May.

It was very much an individualist solution to the problem of poverty and social division, but it involved admitting (a) the poor existed, (b) that there was such a thing as society after all, and (c) that 'individual men and women and families' had responsibilities towards it. Deep down in the engine room of HMS *Thatcherism* it was possible to make out the distant sound of propellors being thrown into reverse.

The Tory Wets, a weak and demoralised faction, had been saying that kind of thing long before their label was invented, but after the 1987 election their arguments against acquisitive individualism began to strike a chord. 'It should not be impossible to infuse this understanding [of the efficacy of market forces] with our more traditional generosity of spirit and to create an enduring English version of Christian Democracy,' wrote Chris Patten, Minister for Overseas Development, in the *Telegraph Sunday Magazine*, 27 September 1987. 'Even in the market place, there must be some who argue that the public library is more important than the video recorder. To borrow from Philip Larkin, there should be more to leave the children than money.'

That was perhaps too direct a criticism of the 'regime' (Mrs Thatcher's word) for a Cabinet minister to make. But Home Secretary Douglas Hurd began to edge back in that direction in his Tamworth speech on 5 February 1988. Hurd, 'a Dry pretending to be a Wet pretending to be a Dry', warned that 'the fruits of our economic success could turn sour unless we can bring back greater social cohesion to our country'. He said disturbances in various shire towns were frequently caused by affluent, white, drunken youths. He blamed the churches' 'sometimes bizarre choice of priorities for discussion', the abdication of teachers who should have helped mould a sense of responsibility and the many parents who 'opted out'.

Then Kenneth Baker ended his Bow Group speech in April – which celebrated the triumph of 'acquisitive individualism' – by saying: 'I do not accept that this drive for self improvement is selfish. However, I do recognise that there is another side to the coin of economic individualism. That other side is social responsibility. Those who succeed have obligations above and beyond that of celebrating their own success.' He went on to praise housing cooperatives, the cooperation involved in neighbourhood watch schemes and businesses' responsibility to their communities. Indeed his speech was entitled 'The Community of Individuals', a coded jibe at those in his party who think the community is a fictitious body.

There was a sort of uneasiness in the air, as Conservative politicians begin to sense that they might not actually have a direct and exclusive channel to the hearts of their electors by virtue of Mrs Thatcher's leadership.

Baker, of course, was once a supporter of Edward Heath, and his Dry, if not individualist, credentials are suspect. But it wasn't just him and Douglas Hurd. Nigel Lawson, chief carrier of the hygroscopic crystals during the monetarist phase, said that same month: 'What I do think is important is that those who are well off should show a sense of social obligation, and I am very glad indeed that since we took office charitable giving has something like doubled in real terms' (*This Week Next Week*, 21 April 1988).

Mrs Thatcher's speech to the Kirk was also strongly individualist (speaking of rescuing the nation 'soul by soul'), but again pointed up the contradiction at the heart of her supposed revolution. She admitted that the Tenth Commandment ('thou shalt not covet') 'recognises that making money and owning things could become selfish activities'. But how can they? Owning things is supposed to engender a sense of responsibility, and her government has tried – with some success, surely? – to 'encourage the best instincts and convictions of the people, instincts and convictions which I am convinced are far more deeply rooted than is often supposed'.

How come, then, her Home Secretary is bemoaning the moral degeneration of the nation? How come 'graciousness has been replaced by surliness in much of everyday life', as Mrs Thatcher herself complained just before her Edinburgh speech (*The Observer*, 1 May 1988)? Is the battle for moral responsibility being won or lost?

Was there a post-war consensus?

Before assessing the alleged triumph of individualism, and the greater sense of moral responsibility that was supposed to go with it, the first half of the national myth needs to be examined more closely. The idea that one dominant mode of thinking (the post-war collectivist consensus) was replaced by another (the Thatcherite individualist hegemony) on 3 May 1979 is obviously a simplification. But was there a 'post-war consensus' from 1945 to 1979?

On this question Peter Jenkins' book is surprisingly ambivalent, considering the finality of its subtitle, 'The Ending of the Socialist Era'. At first, Jenkins says that the idea of a post-war consensus 'was founded more in myth than in reality' (p. 3). The fact that 'full employment and the maintenance of the welfare state became the accepted goals of both parties' (p. 5) hardly suggests that what mythical consensus there might have been was a 'socialist' one. Halfway through the book Jenkins distances himself from the notion of a socialist post-war consensus, commenting that in 1978–81 'some went so far as to say . . . that the Labour Party was in the last throes of a terminal decline, presaging the ending of the socialist era' (p. 105). But, by the end of the book, he revealed himself to be one of these anonymous soothsayers: 'The Socialist Age was coming to an end. Across the whole swathe of northern Europe the mode of politics which had dominated the postwar period, and much of the twentieth century, was in decline' (p. 335).

Mainly, this confusion comes about because he doesn't distinguish between a *coup d'étàt* (as he calls Mrs Thatcher's capture of the Tory party leadership) in the institutions of British politics and a transformation of public opinion.

Professor Nicholas Deakin debunked the idea of a 'post-war consensus' lasting in public opinion beyond 1948 in an essay published in February 1988. The argument that there was a post-war consensus, arising out of the experience of the war and the memory of the 1930s depression, is, he said: 'at its most convincing between the acceptance of the Beveridge proposals in 1943 and the completion of the structure of welfare in 1948, with an afterglow persisting into the middle 1950s among politicians, and a permanent lodgment in the popular consciousness which not even the experience of the 1980s has fully eradicated.'

The policies of nationalisation and government planning of the 1945–51 Labour government were

> assailed with vigour by the Conservative opposition and above all in the Tory press, who found and fully exploited a rich vein in gibes at the rationing system with its regimented equality and at the snoopers and jacks-in-office who allegedly operated it. Beaverbrook and his fellow press lords tapped increased public weariness over continuing austerity, five years after the victorious end to the war. Churchill responded to many of these trends in opinion, arguing forcefully against the continued use of controls, which, he maintained, had been preserved 'to give the government that power of interference in the daily life of the country which is a characteristic of socialism'. But he reserved his most vehement criticism for the government's nationalisation legislation, which he characterised as 'borrowed from foreign lands and alien minds'.

Deakin argues that there was a limited 'convergence' among politicians, however, a centre-ward move by elements of the Conservative Party, led by R. A. Butler. The important factor was Butler's 'achievement in persuading the Conservative Party to accept the continuation of the tripartite approach to economic policy, with a strong role for the unions and a degree of government intervention in industry'.

Butler recast Tory party policies as head of the Research Department which Churchill created after his defeat in 1945. Butler said he believed that, 'as in the days of Peel, the Conservatives must be seen to have accommodated themselves to a social revolution'. The centrepiece was a new economic strategy called the 'Industrial Charter' of which he later wrote: 'Our first purpose was to counter the charge and the fear that we were the party of industrial go-as-you-please and devil-take-the-hindmost, that full employment and the welfare state were not safe in our hands.' According to Deakin, 'the passage of the charter by a bewildered party conference signalled formal adoption of the economic programme; on social policy the emphasis was not merely on continuity with the [wartime] coalition's programme but ownership of it, with references to the "new social services" as "mainly our own handiwork" '.

Only on the National Health Service, where Aneurin Bevan departed from the wartime coalition's script, was there serious opposition in parliament on a question of social policy. So, although the Tory party and press remained vigorously opposed to nationalisation and planning, Butler had shifted the Tory party's position on full employment, trade unions and the welfare state to such an extent that, when he took office as Chancellor in 1951, his policies 'can justly be characterised as consensus-based'.

Butler's hold over the Conservative Party was only broken in the party's 'abrupt shift to the right before the 1970 election', which Edward Heath 'fought on the Selsdon manifesto, indistinguishable in many respects from Margaret Thatcher's of ten years later'.[7] Which means that, on the central questions of full employment, trade unions and the welfare state, there *was* effectively a consensus from 1943 to 1970. But Deakin's important point is that it was a much more selective consensus than is often thought, and was limited to Westminster politicians (many of them reluctant) rather than representing public opinion as a whole.

And the reasons for the break-up of even that limited consensus in the late 1960s and the 1970s were not necessarily to do with the inadequacies of collectivism. 'The problems of the 1970s perhaps stemmed from too little rather than too much collectivism in British industrial relations,' according to John MacInnes in *Thatcherism at Work*.

Many of the troubles governments faced in the 1970s stemmed from their attempts to maintain full employment as a priority. In abandoning this goal Thatcherism has had its greatest impact on the British industrial relations system; not by undermining trade union bargaining power but by taking the unemployed out of the reckoning and letting employers and workers maximise their own returns regardless of the consequences for the aggregate level of employment. (p. xiv)

This analysis of what happened in the 1970s is supported by David Marquand in *The Unprincipled Society*:

Keynesian demand management had become unworkable partly because the trade-off between inflation and unemployment had deteriorated. Yet a long-term incomes policy, on the lines of the incomes policies followed in some of the 'neo-corporatist' social democracies of Scandinavia and central Europe, might have offset that deterioration. [But] such a policy would have required different attitudes to collective bargaining . . . and, most of all, a different view of the proper relationship between the state and organised labour and capital. The full employment commitment of postwar Keynesian social democracy was undermined, not by economic imperatives, but by moral and political preferences, and by the institutions which embodied and transmitted past moral and political preferences. (p. 210)

MacInnes and Marquand argue that 1945 marked a triumph of collectivism which was never complete enough to overcome the earlier traditions. Some of those earlier traditions reasserted themselves remarkably quickly. Further nationalisation was already massively unpopular by 1948 (see chapter 7, p. 102). But other collectivist traditions, this book argues, have survived and continue to thrive among ordinary people despite a dramatic switch in the philosophy of the Conservative Party at Westminster.

The tradition of individualism

The idea that the primary political conflict in Britain is between individualism and collectivism is at least a hundred years old, although other 'isms' such as liberalism, conservatism and socialism

15

have usually been used to describe them. The founding of the Fabian Society in 1884 inaugurated a period when the word 'collectivism' was much used to describe a form of socialism distinct from Marxist or other revolutionary doctrines. Its leading figures were Sidney and Beatrice Webb, who hoped their brand of collectivism would permeate the Liberal Party – or both the Liberal and the Conservative parties – until as late as 1912, when they threw in their lot with the rising Labour Party. The Webbs' collectivism remained focused on the state rather than the labour movement as the agency required to carry it out. With votes for women not yet won, the very notion of the democratic state was still new and liberating.

'Forward with collectivism' is not much of a rallying cry, but the Webbs explicitly founded the *New Statesman* in 1913 to 'welcome . . . the world movement towards collectivism'. The First World War seemed to put paid to that kind of language, although their strand of Fabian socialism, heavily imbued with a Liberal inheritance, remained identifiably intact, gathering strength until its political triumph in 1945, with the nationalisation of major industries and the creation of state education, health and welfare services.

If the Webbs, the *New Statesman* and most of the infant Labour Party were promoting collectivism, then what they were against was the individualism of the status quo, or what the Webbs called the 'statecraft of pecuniary self interest'. In terms uncannily similar to the obituaries for collectivism in the 1980s, the Webbs declared in 1913:

Apart from personal preference for the motive of serving the community over that of the desire for personal riches, the Socialists assert that the statecraft of pecuniary self interest is today seen to have failed. Not in this country alone, but in all the lands of civilised industrialism, the motive of desire for riches demonstrably fails to make the best of the country's natural resources. On the contrary, the adoption of this statecraft demonstrably results in the continuance, if not in the intensifying, of the penury, the degradation and the demoralisation in which the mass of manual workers are sunk.[8]

The word individualism had begun to be used in a political sense half a century earlier. And it is apt that it should have been condemned at its birth as nothing more than a cerebral form of selfishness – by a conservative. '*Individualism* is a novel expression, to which a novel idea has given birth,' wrote Alexis de Tocqueville in 1835.

> Our fathers were acquainted only with *egoism* . . . Individualism is a mature and calm feeling, which disposes each member of the community to sever himself from the mass of his fellows . . . Selfishness blights the germ of all virtue; individualism, at first, only saps the virtues of public life; but in the long run, it attacks and destroys all others, and is at length absorbed in downright selfishness. Selfishness is a vice as old as the world, which does not belong to one form of society more than to another: individualism is of democratic origin, and it threatens to spread in the same ratio as the equality of condition.[9]

De Tocqueville points up two things that are still essential ingredients of individualism today. One is that it is not just the same as a belief in free-market economics; the other is that it has something to do with democracy. De Tocqueville believed that democracy actually causes individualism, and disapproved of both, but it would be safer now to say simply that Thatcherite individualism is compatible with democracy. Modern individualism is associated with the claim of a dispersal of political power: the Conservative slogan of 'power to the people'. The relationship of modern Tory individualism with free-market economics is also ambiguous. It endorses individual free enterprise, for instance – but not necessarily international finance capital or large corporations.

What does individualism mean?

For at least 150 years, then, individualism has been an identifiable strand of popular political values. But in order to assess whether it has 'triumphed' in the 1980s, it must be defined more precisely. The attempt to define individualism reveals some of the difficulties of using 'individualism versus collectivism' as a way of looking at ideology at the popular level.

The main problem is that poles of the axis are not necessarily seen by non-philosophers as opposites or contradictions: as the following chapter show, support for individualist values can co-exist with deeply held collectivist convictions. Neil Kinnock's collectivism is a 'platform' for individualism; for him, collectivism comes first, as a *precondition* of individual freedom and self-development, whereas Conservatives put individualism first, as the precondition of collective advancement. But ordinary people will use and support individual *and* collective services (for example, private health insurance *and* the National Health Service), without necessarily seeing any ideological conflict between them.

Furthermore, the left-wing version of the triumph of individualism is in many ways simply a rephrasing of the disgust at the greed of modern materialism and the lament for past altruism that has always attended the idea of a past golden age. That there is nothing new in this is demonstrated by de Tocqueville.

More recently, Daniel Bell observed in the 1970s, in *The Cultural Contradictions of Capitalism*, that the hallmark of the late twentieth century is the 'loss of *civitas*, that spontaneous willingness to obey the law, to respect the rights of others, to forgo the temptations of private enrichment at the expense of the public weal – in short to honour the "city" of which one is a member' (p. 245).

Complaints about the greed of the average person are part of a wider confusion over the nature of 1980s' individualism, which can be broken down into three elements: there is the confusion of self-interest with a belief in free-market economics; of a desire for self-reliance with a rejection of collectivism; and of increased buying power with a political preference for private provision.

To take those confusions one by one, if people feel it is in their interest to have inflation brought down at the cost of others' jobs, or to have an operation done privately instead of waiting for the NHS, then they will vote or pay accordingly, but the meaning of their choice cannot necessarily be interpreted as an endorsement of individualism or a rejection of collectivism. People may actually prefer the collectivist option (low inflation plus low unemployment, or more resources for the NHS), but accept the 'individualist' option as second best if it is not available.

Secondly, as the Labour MP David Blunkett was quick to point out after the 1987 election, self-reliance doesn't have to exclude relying on others, though he realised that the Labour Party was riddled with misconceptions on this point.

Although it may be misinterpreted to say so quite so starkly, democratic socialists should be appealing to the very instincts which Thatcherite Conservatism has attempted to take to its soul. Not the instincts of selfishness and greed, of materialism and self assertion, but those instincts which are deep-rooted in the communities which made Labour great – beliefs in self reliance and self determination; a desire to have the dignity of looking after yourself and not having the state or local bureaucracy telling you what to do or how to do it. (*The Independent*, 7 July 1987)

Thirdly, just because there has been a steady rise in real incomes and wealth for most of the population, enabling many more people to afford a home of their own, private health insurance, private education, a few shares and a personal pension, does not necessarily mean that more people endorse private provision as a general political principle. Of course, the better-off are more likely to have individualist political values than the less well-off; but the determining factor is not money, it is class. And in fact it is the social class with the lowest average male income that is most strongly individualist in its politics. On average, self-employed and small business men earn 4 per cent less than manual workers, although on average 60 per cent adopted 'free enterprise' positions on nationalisation, equality, job creation, trade unions and private schools in 1983, as against 32 per cent of manual workers. [10]

With these distractions cleared away, individualism can be reduced to a simple proposition. It represents a desire for, and a belief in the moral superiority of, greater independence – for more control over work, home and social role – which is seen as *necessarily* rejecting the need to depend on others. It is not enough to say that individualists would 'go private' if they could afford it; they must also support in some way the idea that market provision is a better way for services to be provided generally. But individualism is not a political philosophy. It is subpolitical, an attitude that exists below the level of a systematic programme of public policy; or even anti-political, in the sense that politics pertains by definition to people collectively.

A central feature of individualism is that it denotes a particular and emotive attitude to society: it denies its existence. 'There's no such thing as society,' Mrs Thatcher said in October 1987. 'There are individual men and women and there are families'(*Woman's Own*, 31 October 1987).

However, individualism provides the main root of a political philosophy, that of the free-market conservatism, which holds that all possible goods and services (including labour) should be provided and consumed privately through priced transactions between autonomous individuals (or families). This political philosophy *does* acknowledge the fact of society, and argues that the pursuit of individual interests leads automatically to a better and richer community – that 'self love and social' are the same.

Individualism is an impulse that also features strongly in other political philosophies. Anarchism rejects the state more strongly, and radical liberalism, or libertarianism, lays similar stress on the individual. It was Jeremy Bentham, in 1780, who described the community as a 'fictious body'.[11] However, the utilitarian liberal tradition which he founded also tends to stress economic equality, a goal which requires collective action. As a moral value, individualism conflicts both with the value of equality and with the value of 'tradition'. Hence its ambiguity, sometimes seeming to have more in common with the radical philosophies of the Left than with the paternalist philosophy of the old Burkeian Tory party.

What constitutes triumph?

This investigation is not concerned with political philosophy, however, but with popular political values, and values are not easy quantities to measure. How do you draw conclusions about what 'ordinary people' as a whole think, whether the consensus shifted to left or right, or from collective to individual values? How are political beliefs structured? One of the reasons why individualism appears triumphant is because it is the values and propaganda of politicians, and especially government politicians, that dominate the media. The values of ordinary people are almost always interpreted through politicians and commentators.

The best way to find out what people think is to ask them. Or some of them. This book uses two techniques: representative opinion surveys to quantify attitudes and changes in them, and in-depth interviews to gauge the texture, interconnections and meanings of what people say.

20

The first thing the triumphalists have to establish is that the new individualism is different from 'ordinary' support for the Conservative Party. In particular, it has to be distinguished from the long British tradition of working-class Toryism. David Selbourne, author of *Against Socialist Illusion*, has no doubt that Thatcherite Conservatism is different.

> Labour has been worsted three times by a brand of Toryism with a deep reach into the very constituency to which Labour is appealing. It is in essence a working class Toryism of thrift and family privacy, 'independence', patriotism and self reliance. This is a politics which seems so 'ordinary', even classless, that millions of equally 'ordinary' people – Labour's own – have no difficulty in identifying with it. (*The Independent*, 22 July 1987)

A more sophisticated idea, identified with the Eurocommunist magazine *Marxism Today*, is that of the 'hegemony' of Thatcherism.[12] This suggests that support for Mrs Thatcher's Conservatives is not merely electoral, but that a new (individualist) ideology has come to dominate the language and institutions of politics, including all sorts of areas of life not usually thought of as being political, such as popular culture, leisure and shopping. The implication is that Conservative voting is the just part of the expression of a new, enduring consensus.

However, if this were the case, the Conservatives should have done exceptionally well in the three elections in which this hegemony, or new 'brand of Toryism', has allegedly held sway.

The triumph of individualism is clearly not the same thing as an electoral triumph for Mrs Thatcher's Conservative Party. Her victories in 1983 and 1987 were less landslides than cases of subsidence between a divided opposition. It is true that the Conservatives did unusually badly in the two 1974 elections, and so the conversion of the electorate to individualism in 1979 could have made up for a decline in 'traditional' Conservative support. Indeed, the New Right coterie that effected Margaret Thatcher's leadership coup in 1975 argued precisely that. They asserted that the Conservative Party had seriously lost its way in 1974, and urgently needed ideological renewal (although no one talked at the time of the hegemony of Wilsonism). And in crude terms of numbers of votes,

10**Table 1**   The Conservative Vote, 1945 to 1987

	Conservatives	Non-Conservatives
1945	39.6	60.4
1950	43.4	56.6
1951	48.0	52.0
1955	49.7	50.3
1959	49.4	50.6
1964	43.4	56.6
1966	41.9	58.1
1970	46.4	53.6
1974 Feb	37.9	62.1
1974 Oct	35.8	64.2
1979	43.9	56.1
1983	42.4	57.6
1987	42.3	57.7

Percentages, United Kingdom

if Conservatism was hegemonic from 1979 to 1987, then it was also so from 1950 to 1964 and in 1970 – exactly the period when, according to Kenneth Baker, 'we were all collectivists then'.

Indeed, nearly a year after the election which marked the 'social transformation' of Bruce Anderson's 'petit-bourgeois revolution', Anderson himself noticed that

> the economic progress of recent years, plus the increased numbers and confidence of the middle class, put the Conservatives' electoral success in a new, unflattering perspective. They should be doing much better: there is a strong case to be made that in relying on a divided opposition to win elections on 42 per cent of the vote, the Tories are seriously under-performing. Given the political demography of Britain, this government should be winning the support of well over 50 per cent of the voters. (*Sunday Telegraph*, 17 April 1988)

The New Right thesis is still logically possible. It is possible that, if the end of collectivism had not propelled Mrs Thatcher to power and had not the triumph of individualism kept her in office, the Conservatives would have performed even less well in the last three elections. But it would be a strange sort of triumph which was only great enough to enable its architect to hang on to the average Conservative vote since the war.

No. If there has been a triumph of individualism, then it has to have been of the 'hegemonic' variety, but with the main beneficiary in the centre ground of politics: the Liberal, Alliance and Democrat parties. It would be paradoxical if the party which articulated the values of the Thatcher Revolution most stridently and claimed its victory merely managed 'ordinary' electoral success. But this is not an entirely outlandish suggestion. Mrs Thatcher made much at the Tory conference in October 1987 of the opposition's alleged adoption of individualism: 'Right up to the 11th of June, the Labour Party, the Liberals and the SDP were busy saying that Conservatism doesn't work. Oddly enough, since the 12th of June, they've been saying that it does. And so our political opponents are now feverishly packaging their policies to look like ours.' It could be that the rise of individualism is an all-party phenomenon, explaining the transformation of the Conservative Party from a patrician club to a free-market think tank, the growth of third-party politics and the survival of the new-look, slightly individualist Labour Party, brain-dead as Norman Tebbit thinks it is. The Tories' lack of overwhelming success could then be explained by the fact that the other two parties are also individualist.

Or it could be that there are now two individualist parties, the Tories and the centre party, vanquishing the collectivist Labour Party. In which case the real political triumph was won by the Alliance in 1983, winning a quarter of the popular vote, and that tide was already ebbing by 1987. But the individualist credentials of the centre party are doubtful, especially with the eclipse of David Owen.

In measuring political values, most social scientists concentrate on equality versus 'free enterprise', which is a useful substitute for collectivism versus individualism. Labour supporters tend to believe in economic equality, and Conservatives in 'free enterprise', with Democrats about halfway in between. Centre-party supporters tend to be neither strongly collectivist nor individualist. Of course, the growth of third-party voting at Labour's expense would, if other things were equal, herald a marginal shift in emphasis towards individualism in society generally. But other things are not equal. The growth of the third party occurred independently of egalitarian values, which didn't change.

The spread of higher education and changes in class composition could make sense of a claim that the triumph of individualism consisted of the long-term decline of the Labour Party. Indeed, it might have been expected that, as the Labour Party is the most collectivist of the three parties, and the manual working class the most collectivist social class in its values, the entire post-war period has been the era of the Decline of Collectivism. This is the only plausible part of Peter Jenkins' thesis: not 'Mrs Thatcher's Revolution' but 'The Ending of the Socialist Era'. It would be plausible if the recession of 1980–1 had catalysed many of the effects of that long decline, so that the 1980s heralded the defeat of collectivism even if it did not signal the triumph of specifically Thatcherite individualism.

But no. It simply has not happened. Although the shrinking of the manual working class is the single most important explanation of the twenty-year decline in the Labour vote from the 48–49 per cent achieved in 1945, 1951 and 1966, it hasn't been accompanied by a decline in collectivist attitudes. On the basis of the continuing expansion of the more Conservative social classes, individualist values should have become more prevalent since 1979. That they have not suggests not only that the Thatcher Revolution didn't happen, but that Margaret Thatcher has only managed to stand still with the advantage of social change on her side. The growth of a more-or-less 'collectivist' centre-party vote is an index of the failure of the Thatcher Revolution.

The evidence of opinion surveys is that there has been no underlying change in egalitarian values in the 1980s. On most issues which have anything to do with what might be called 'values', attitudes have been stable during the 1980s; however, there has been an increase in support for women's rights, a decline in support for the death penalty and a shift towards authoritarianism on the issue of homosexuality. It has been a very strange Revolution.

The evidence

So far, it seems, almost all the political debate has been conducted in a sort of evidence-free zone. This book draws on two main kinds of evidence: opinion surveys of representative samples of the population, and in-depth interviews with smaller numbers of people, mostly conducted specially for the purpose.

The British Social Attitudes survey is the best source of accurate, quantifiable information about the attitudes and values that lie behind the 'public opinion' of the political media. Its great strength is that it is an annual survey which can measure change over time by asking a consistent series of questions. Its main drawback is that it began only in 1983, and so doesn't reveal how attitudes changed in the early, turbulent Thatcher years. However, its directors have made an effort where possible to use identical questions to those asked previously in other surveys and by other polling organisations. In particular, many of the questions are linked with the British Election Studies polls, which are carried out by the same independent research institiute (Social and Community Planning Research), and whose advisors and directors overlap.

The British Election Studies are a series of opinion surveys carried out immediately after each General Election since 1964, with some panel surveys in between elections. Much of the distilled wisdom of this long-running series is contained in *How Britain Votes*, by Anthony Heath, Roger Jowell and John Curtice, which reports the results of the 1983 study. (The same authors intend to publish a sequel, containing the results of the 1987 study, in 1989.)

The commercial polling organisations also carry out a huge volume of research which frequently yields comparisons over time. I have drawn especially on the work of Gallup, which has some consistent series of questions going back to 1937, and Market Opinion Research International (MORI).

The ability to measure changes in public opinion over time is crucial to this book's argument that individualism has not triumphed. Too many assertions about what the British are now like are based on one-off surveys. To take a typical example, in May 1988 the market research company Mintel produced a report on 'Youth Lifestyles', costing £550, which claimed: 'Ten years of Tory rule have seen some of the most profound changes in living memory among the younger generation. Young people are more individualistic in style.' But Mintel's survey did not repeat the same questions as an earlier one, so there is no way of knowing whether young people have always been 'individualistic in style'. It may be true that 'a new generation of thoroughly pragmatic realists, far from rejecting or rebelling against the values of the highly consumer-oriented society in which they have grown up, aspire above all to take their place as responsible adults and to enjoy the benefits of adult status'. But Mintel's survey did not prove it. It is quite possible that a similar survey in 1978 would have shown that the previous generation was exactly the same.

Large opinion surveys (the British Social Attitudes survey interviews 3,000 people every year) are able to produce reasonably accurate measurements of the views of the whole population by using random sampling techniques, and two such surveys can measure the extent of change over time. What they can't say, however, is *how* people answered the questions, what conditions they wanted to attach to their answers, which questions they thought were unfair or meaningless, and what they thought the questions or their answers actually meant.

These are the sorts of things that can only be found out by talking directly to the people concerned. We didn't need to interview 3,000 people for this book, because the survey information is already available. What was required was a smaller sample of people who were typical rather than representative. The focus of this book is also narrower than the whole population; the strategic social territory which has allegedly been annexed by the victorious forces of individualism is the affluent working class. So the interviews for this book concentrate on working-class people who used to vote Labour. Of course, this means that the book is biased, in that the voices in the following chapters are mostly those of Conservative or Alliance voters. This bias is kept in check by the overview of quantitative survey findings.

The main individual interviews were carried out by my colleague Jane Ratford in Putney, South London, and in Basildon, Essex, in November and December 1987. I interviewed ex-Labour voters in Wolverhampton in December 1987 and former and current Labour voters in Glasgow, in February 1988. People on the electoral register were selected at random and asked about their job and voting history, and working-class ex-Labour voters were interviewed in their homes for up to an hour. We used an open-ended questionnaire (Appendix 1) to guide the interviews, but allowed interviewees to explain and add to their answers.

The other in-depth interviews conducted for this book were two group discussions in Roehampton, South London, in February 1988. The participants, one group of eight women and one of six men, were recruited at random from skilled and non-manual working-class (social classes C1 and C2) parents aged 25 to 44, who had voted Labour but who voted Conservative or Alliance in 1987. The groups were convened by Deborah Mattinson, a director of marketing consultancy Gould Mattinson Associates, and a convenor of the 'Shadow Communications Agency' – the Labour Party's answer to Saatchi and Saatchi in the 1987 election. Discussion groups are now widely used by advertisers, corporate image-makers and even trade unions; they help fill out the individual picture by giving a feel for the way people express their views in a 'social' setting, and how they react to other opinions. In order that the reader can check the vote, occupation and family circumstances of the individuals quoted in later chapters, an index of all the interviewees is given on pp. 175–88 (Appendix 2).

In addition to these two sources of 'ordinary' people's voices, I commissioned a report from Gould Mattinson Associates which summarised research carried out in the months after the 1987 General Election. The report covers telephone interviews and group discussions carried out between June and October.

Lastly, some use is made of a report of discussion groups carried out by Penny Horner of the Consumer Connection Ltd, commissioned by the London Labour Party in an attempt to find out why Labour lost the Battersea constituency in 1987. These groups consisted of lapsed Labour voters living on council estates (including owners), aged 25 to 48 and in the manual working class (C2 and D).

The book uses these sources of information to argue that there has been no shift towards individualism in the 1980s, although there has been a rise in some 'liberal' values and an increase in political self-confidence since the 1950s – largely because of the spread of higher education.

2
Overview

How can something as intangible as 'individualism' be measured? Chapter 1 defines individualism as the desire for control that excludes others. It is represented in the desire to 'go private' in education, housing and health care, and is generalised as political support for a system of private provision for everyone. Individualism rejects trade unions, is hostile to social security (especially universal benefits) and accents individual material prosperity rather than social goods.

The following chapters investigate attitudes to each of these issues in turn, but that investigation is complicated by the fact that, in each case, attitudes are affected by changes in circumstances. Attitudes often appear to be becoming more collectivist because the Conservative government has moved the goalposts, so that anyone who was happy with the status quo in 1979 could appear to have become more left wing since then. So there is a need to test for individualism in the abstract, to dig beneath the surface of immediate political issues in an attempt to tap underlying values.

The British Election Study of the 1979 election (*Decade of Dealignment*) claimed to have identified a 'rightward shift in electoral opinion' over the period of the 1974–9 Labour government. Unfortunately it used just two questions to support this claim: one on nationalisation and one on 'social services and benefits'. It is true that the proportion favouring further nationalisation fell from 30 per cent in 1974 to 16 per cent in 1979, but in the interim the government had nationalised British Leyland and much of the aerospace and shipbuilding industries. Similarly the increase from 38 to 49 in the percentage of those thinking that 'social services and benefits have gone too far' is not unexpected as a retrospective judgement on the

28

respective records of the Heath and Wilson–Callaghan administrations.[1]

The British Election Study of the 1983 election (*How Britain
Votes*) was much more careful, and identified two dimensions of
political values – economic equality and social liberalism. But the
question on income redistribution used by *How Britain Votes* to
test the electorate's egalitarianism is dogged by changes in question
wording (see below, p. 33), so its conclusion that the electorate
had moved to the right on the issue of equality since 1974 has to
be treated with caution.[2]

The reports of the British Social Attitudes surveys take this kind
of analysis of popular values further, but only since 1983, when
they claim to have discovered a shift in the opposite direction.
One of the authors of *How Britain Votes*, John Curtice, used
the much wider range of questions in the British Social Attitudes
surveys to show how the electorate had now appeared to shift to
the left on many of the issues which divide the Conservative and
Labour Parties.

Between 1983 and 1985 there was a marked fall in the numbers
of people agreeing with a series of 'right-wing' statements:

	1983	*1985*
	%	%
Britain should keep its nuclear weapons	77	68
The government should not reduce spending on defence	53	42
Government should give highest priority to keeping down inflation [rather than] keeping down unemployment	27	22
There should not be more state ownership of industry	49	31
The welfare state makes people nowadays less willing to look after themselves	52	44

Curtice concluded that if there had been an earlier shift to the
right on the principle of equality, it had been reversed since the
1983 election:

It does appear that the electorate has been moving significantly
away from much of the ideological ground staked out by the
present government. The fall in Conservative partisanship [in
1985] . . . appears to signify a decline in support for the values

29

of the Conservative Party, a decline which is likely to be more enduring than an unfavourable evaluation of the government's current economic performance.[3]

But, again, several of the questions fall victim to the 'moving goalposts' fallacy. The questions on nuclear weapons and defence spending do seem to indicate a genuine shift in the public's views (which will have been influenced by the rapprochement between President Reagan and General Secretary Gorbachev and the anti-nuclear backlash of the Chernobyl disaster). However, they have little to do with individualism. In the case of each of the other three questions, which are much more to do with individualism and collectivism, the circumstances have changed, and so a 'shift to the left' would be expected even if people's underlying attitudes remained exactly the same. Unemployment, although falling, remains high, while the memory of high inflation has receded and inflation appears under control, so more people are likely to accord a higher priority to the battle against unemployment. Similarly, the privatisation programme sold off the obvious candidates first, so people are more likely to think the process has gone far enough, or that selling off natural monopolies like British Telecom and British Gas is going too far.

The last question, on the welfare state, is the most abstract of the questions and one which most seems to tap an individualist value. Unfortunately for Curtice, it became clear afterwards that it was probably affected by a statistical blip. Because opinion surveys are subject to random error, every now and then a figure will be out of line by chance, and this seems to be one of them. The proportion agreeing that 'the welfare state makes people nowadays less willing to look after themselves' was 51 per cent in 1984, and then, after Curtice wrote, 50 per cent in 1986 and 52 per cent in 1987. The 44 per cent figure in 1985 seems to be a 'rogue', with the real level of agreement unchanged between 1983 and 1987. (The 1986 figures for the other questions confirm the apparent leftward trend, with agreement falling a further 1 or 2 percentage points, except on nuclear weapons which shifted back rightwards by just 1 point to 69 per cent.)

But even if the 'shift to the left' was exaggerated, one thing is perfectly clear from these figures: that, since 1983 at least, there has been no shift to the right in the basic political outlook of the electorate.

Curtice's other problem was the outcome of the 1987 election. So much, the electors seemed to say, for the British Social Attitudes survey. In the 1987 British Social Attitudes report, he wrote: 'Mrs Thatcher's re-election in June 1987 is surely ample proof that the British electorate has shifted decisively to the right. 'Or is it?'[4] He analysed the 'value' of equality in greater detail and investigated its links with political loyalties and demonstrated conclusively that people's views of the economy affect the way they vote without affecting their underlying values. So in the short term (even a period of several years – and the Conservatives have presided over steadily rising living standards for up to three-quarters of the population since 1982) it is possible for governments to override the electorate's basic values by delivering the economic goods.

Although the swing in support back to the Conservative Party in the run-up to the 1987 election didn't reflect a change in underlying values, Curtice's analysis confirmed the importance of the value of economic equality in distinguishing between Conservative and Labour supporters. Of the fifteen statements which separated left and right most sharply in 1985 and 1986, all but one ('The siting of American nuclear missiles in Britain makes Britain a less safe place') were to do with economic equality.[5]

However, the fourteen 'egalitarian' statements do not represent one homogeneous value. They all contain an element of class consciousness ('There is one law for the rich, one law for the poor'), but eleven of them also contain an explicit 'collectivist' element, either supporting the role of government ('The government should spend more money to get rid of poverty') or trade unions ('Employees need strong trade unions to protect their interests') in securing equality. This last statement is the one on which Conservative and Labour supporters differed most of all: half of all Conservatives disagreed, while one in ten Labour supporters did. It is also the one which combines class consciousness and collectivism most forcefully (trade unions being a more immediate expression of collective identity than the state), and which least stresses equality.

In fact, what is striking about these statements is that they are not egalitarian in principle so much as an expression of class interest. They confirm that class, and not independent and abstract or moral 'values' (such as lie behind opposition to American nuclear missiles), is the most important factor in British politics.

It could be argued – indeed, it often is – that the new individualism is breaking up old class loyalties, that materialism and political selfishness are acting like solvents on the bonds of working-class solidarity, and that class politics is dying in Britain as a result. Not true. *How Britain Votes*, the study of the 1983 election, proves that class remains the basis of division between Labour and Conservative voters. What has happened is that the third party vote has increased in all classes, and so the strongholds of the working-class Labour vote and the middle-class Tory vote are smaller than they would otherwise be.[6]

The picture is complicated, and different interpretations of it resulted in one of the greatest academic disputations of recent political science. Ivor Crewe of Essex University argued that a process of 'class dealignment' has been happening since the early 1960s. But the authors of *How Britain Votes*, Heath, Jowell and Curtice, show that there is no consistent decline in the extent to which Labour voting is concentrated in the working class as opposed to the middle class (and Tory voting vice versa) between 1964 and 1983.[7]

The picture is further complicated by the fact that the manual working class is shrinking, so the core Labour vote has been doubly eroded, while the core Tory vote is sustained by the expansion of middle-class occupations. (These questions are looked at in more depth in Chapter 9.)

Was 1979 a turning point?

So much, then, for the triumph of individualist values during Margaret Thatcher's second term. But what about the overall picture since 1979? What about the alleged decline of collectivism during the 1970s? If the divided opposition explains Mrs Thatcher's dominance since 1979, how did the Conservatives come to power in the first place? Surely something happened? Did not the political ground shift under Jim Callaghan's feet? Well, no. The Labour government was seen as a failure, as stumbling from crisis to crunch. This was not simply a failing of public relations, it reflected

Labour's specific lack of an answer to the contradiction between the interests of the state and its employees. The public sector strikes of the 'Winter of Discontent' (1978–9) and the public spending crisis of 1976–9 were the symptoms of a crisis in the economics of collectivism in one country at one time. They did not betoken a loss of faith in collectivist values, nor were they a demonstration of the bankruptcy of collectivism as a political system. Sweden, Austria and West Germany demonstrate that state collectivism can be stable and successful. And Reagan's America has demonstrated that huge public borrowing is not uniquely the product of collectivism.

There may have been a change of political fashion in the precincts of Westminster and its media compound in 1979, but there is no evidence of a parallel shift in popular attitudes. Unfortunately, only two of Curtice's fourteen 'egalitarian' statements have been asked in anything like a comparable form over the years. And one of the two is rather less than explicitly collectivist: 'Income and wealth should be redistributed towards ordinary working people.' The assumption behind this question is, however, that the transfer of resources should be effected by society collectively through the tax and benefit system, and there has been no change in the majority supporting it during the 1980s. The question wording used by the British Election Studies has changed and Gallup obtains different answers to an identical question but, if an average is taken, the level of agreement was unchanged at 52 per cent between 1979 and 1983–7.[8]

A leftward shift on this question might have been expected because of the growing inequality of income and wealth since 1979. Certainly there has been a growing feeling that government policy is inegalitarian, but there is also evidence that people don't see their *relative* position as being very different.[9] And analysis of answers to similar opinion poll questions shows that responses are particularly unstable and sensitive to changes in wording.[10] However, this is certainly not evidence of a shift away from egalitarianism, let alone collectivism.

The other statement is: 'The government should get rid of private education in Britain.' This reflects the class value of equality in a different way, one which ought to reflect the new individualist aspiration to 'go private'. The proportion wanting to abolish private schools outright appeared to fall from 26 per cent in 1973 to 20 per cent in 1987, but again the question wording is slightly different: in 1987 people were allowed the answer 'It doesn't matter', a sentiment with which 17 per cent agreed.[11] The British Social Attitudes survey allows people to say whether the government 'definitely should' or 'probably should' get rid of private education; this reduced the hard core abolitionists to about 10 per cent, but if the 'probablies' are added, then 27 per cent were still opposed to private education in 1987.[12] So, again, there has been no clear shift towards individualism, even on this quintessentially individualist issue.

The following chapters examine opinion survey evidence on attitudes to housing, health care, trade unions, social security, nationalisation versus privatisation and tax in more depth. But there is a striking lack of opinion poll evidence going back in a consistent series before 1983 on any question which meaningfully tests individualism as a *general* political principle, and which is not affected by a changing context.

A question like 'The welfare state makes people nowadays less willing to look after themselves' really goes to the heart of the new Tory individualism. But this question wasn't asked in the 1970s; it is one of the questions first asked by the British Social Attitudes survey in 1983 – although it is important to have established that responses to it haven't changed since then. In order to guess at attitudes before 1983 an analogy can be made with another question that has been asked both by Gallup and by the British Election Studies. The percentage thinking that 'the welfare benefits that are available today have gone too far' rose during the period of the 1974–9 Labour government, but has since fallen to a much lower level.[13]

	%
1974	34
1978	43
1979	50
1981	25
1983	20
1987	16

Clearly, this is another case in which the 'goalposts' have moved. The decline in the numbers thinking benefits had 'gone too far' since 1979 was influenced by the massive rise in unemployment in the early 1980s (see Chapter 8), in a way the more abstract question about the welfare state 'making people less willing to look after themselves' might not have been. However, the one conclusion to which these figures do *not* point is that individualist attitudes to welfare are tightening their grip on the hearts and minds of the nation.

A completely different approach to the quest for (more) rampant individualism would be to look more generally for any signficant long-term changes in public opinion that could be to do with enduring values, and to see how these might be related to the alleged increase in selfishness or self-reliance. Data from the British Election Studies can be combined with Gallup poll findings to produce several reliable series on attitudes to social issues over time (as is done in Chapter 10). However, the only clear value-related shifts in people's attitudes since the mid-1970s to be thrown up by this scatter-gun approach are the rise in support for women's rights, the decline in support for the death penalty and increased hostility towards homosexuals. This, too, is not the triumph of individualism of which the government's apologists speak.

Nor, indeed, is the one shift in public opinion which could plausibly be described as individualist. Between October 1974 and 1983, there was a significant increase in the majority agreeing that the government should 'give workers more say in running the places where they work', from 56 to 68 per cent.[14] This is not what the government means when it talks of giving individuals more independence at work; it wants them to be independent of their trade unions, not of their employers.

The growing demand for 'a say' is of a piece with the growing self-confidence of the British as citizens. But it is a desire for a democratic say, as equals, rather than for the right to assert one's demands as loudly as possible. Successful collectivist politics will have to be imbued more deeply with the idea of participatory democracy in future, but the evidence is that the values of collectivism are as strong as ever.

3

Education

I'm not pro the comprehensive system. I believe in comprehensive schooling but with grammar schools brought back.

Private education for their children is the aspiration of half of all parents. A MORI survey of parents with children aged 11 to 18 in state schools, in May 1987, found that 48 per cent said they would send their children to a private school if they could afford it; 42 per cent would not, and 11 per cent didn't know.[1] Gould Mattinson claim that almost as great a proportion of working-class parents share this aspiration, with only middle-class Labour voters, usually without children, conspicuously denying it on ideological grounds: 'I just wouldn't do it. It would betray everything I believe,' said one such of their interviewees.[2]

'Even though I disagree with it, I would,' said Mr B, a Labour-inclined non-voter in Putney, when asked if he would send his two young children to private school if he could afford it.

At the end of the day they get a better education, which means that their whole lives should benefit. A private school would probably pay a better salary than the state system to its teachers and the private school would want a better type of teacher. The state system doesn't attract highly qualified teachers. The state system can't just be improved by putting in more money. They have done away with various punishments in schools which I've always thought was a bad thing.

It can't be said for certain whether more people nowadays want to send their children to private schools than used to, because MORI's question hasn't been asked in a consistent series over time. Certainly more people *do* send their children to private school than when the Conservatives came to power in 1979, but not many more. The proportion of schoolchildren who are now at private schools is about 7 per cent; it was about 6 per cent in 1979.

Survey questions about attitudes to private schools have to be looked at in more general terms. The British Social Attitudes survey asked in 1983 and 1986 whether there should be: 'more private schools, about the same number as now, fewer private schools or no private schools at all?' The answers in both years were effectively the same, with about two-thirds preferring the 'no change' option, 19 per cent wanting to reduce or abolish private schools and 11–13 per cent wanting more private schools.[3]

No polling organisation seems to have asked a comparable question consistently before 1983, but a Gallup series covering a decade from 1963 to 1973 implies that attitudes are fairly stable. Gallup asked: 'Do you approve of public schools as they exist in England today or should they be abolished?'

	1963	1965	1967	1968	1973
Approve	58	56	52	57	55
Abolish	23	24	28	25	26
Don't know	19	20	20	17	19

These figures appear to show much stronger opposition to private schools than British Social Attitudes, but Gallup was asking for positive approval of them – forcing those who disapprove but who don't actually think they should be restricted or abolished to choose between 'abolish' and 'don't know'. Only 2 per cent said they didn't know when asked the British Social Attitudes question. Also, incidentally, the wording of Gallup's question must have offended a lot of Scottish respondents, who would be quite happy to have private schools abolished south of the border. This question is also one where the meanings and connotations conjured up by the words 'public' and 'private' (see p. 104) are disrupted by the fact that private schools in England are called 'public schools'. This produces unpredictable eddies that make interpreting opinion poll questions difficult. Gallup's interviewees, for instance, may have been more likely to take against private schools because of the association of 'English public schools' with the class system, archaic uniforms and inherited privilege, whereas the use of the phrase 'private schools' ('private or independent schools' in 1983) by the British Social Attitudes survey may actually be more neutral. Nevertheless, one of my interviewees detected hostile loading in my question as to whether he would send his children to a private school if he could afford it. *'Public* school,' he corrected me. 'Yes I will. I will do. You get it better in every way. I went to a state school and it was a load of rubbish. I learnt far more after I left. All schools should be like public schools' (Mr P, Wolverhampton Conservative).

Mr P's enthusiasm for 'public schools' was unusual in that most of the people we interviewed who thought private schools were 'better' (and our interviewees were evenly divided on that point) recognised that they were very expensive and didn't think that they ever could afford them, or could have afforded them. Instead, private schools provided a benchmark – and probably a largely imaginary one – for their concern with standards in the public sector. They would agree with Mr P in saying: 'All schools should be *like* public schools.'

The half of the population who would use private education if they could afford it are more likely to vote Conservative, not usually because it is part of a right-wing ideology, but because they are more likely to be better off and therefore to think of it as a possibility. Nor was the aspiration to go private very strongly related to party loyalty. The ex-Labour voters interviewed for this book were equally divided about whether they would go private if they could afford it. But all of them also supported the idea of the government spending more on state schools, not out of fellow-feeling for the less fortunate, but out of collective self-interest.

All those who were emphatic about going private if they could expressed a strong feeling that standards in the public sector were unacceptably low. Ms E, an Alliance voter with four grown-up children, said: 'Yes, I would have sent them to private school. The teachers are of a better standard than state schools. There you've got teachers teaching subjects for which they have no qualifications. Standards in teacher training colleges need to be raised. My children went to a state school but I had to pay for extra tuition in English, Maths and French. The teachers at their comprehensive didn't have the qualifications to teach the subjects.'

Her husband, Mr E, who voted Conservative in 1987, agreed:

I would have, yes. I would have known what they were being taught and I would have had a say in what they were being taught. I left school when I was 13 but my standard of education was as good as any child of 16 today. There must be something wrong with the system when you get that. I was trying to decipher a form written by a youngster today. It wasn't even written, it was printed and the printing was terrible, I couldn't even read his name. That's no way to write.

Reading, writing and mathematics are taught very poorly. The standard of teachers is very bad; that's why you now have a bad standard of pupil. There are far too many subjects being taught in schools to the detriment of the three Rs. We were taught the essentials as a basis and on that basis we built. We went to learn the trendy subjects of our times at evening classes and we were able to learn them because we had already learnt to read, write and add up.

Ms F, who voted Conservative 1987 but would now vote Labour, was the mother of four children between the ages of 2 and 21, three of them at home.

I'd definitely send my children to private schools if I could. If you weren't satisfied you could take them out and put them into another school. With state schools you can't get in where you want to. The schools around here are terrible. The education is disgusting. My daughter of 12, who goes to school in Richmond, is doing the same work as my 17-year-old. There's too big a concentration of ethnic minorities in the schools in Putney. They're trying too hard to keep them happy without educating the children. Children who have difficulties with English shouldn't hold back the others. I know that makes me sound very bigoted, but I'm not.

Mr G, a Conservative with a 14-year-old daughter, said: 'In state schools the teachers just don't want to know. They don't get to know a child like they did in my day. Our teachers knew us inside out. I would get more involved if she went to a private school. I keep out of the school she's at now, the teachers make me so angry.'

Most ex-Labour voters believed that the quality of state education would worsen under the Conservatives, according to Gould Mattinson's research after the 1987 General Election. But this tended to reinforce the desire for private education rather than support for the Labour Party. This doesn't necessarily mean that they have been converted to 'individualist' policies, however: although ex-Labour voters were keen on the distant prospect of private education, they were more immediately concerned about increased spending on state schools. This demand for more spending didn't translate into support for Labour because, while they criticised the government for the low level of resources of the state sector, they tended to be even more critical of 'loony left' Labour council policies.

Hence an apparent shift from collectivism to individualism was caused not by Labour defectors becoming more individualistic, but through the politics of sex and race.

While most of the people who would go private if they could said so because of poor standards in the public sector, there were also a few who used the more speculative 'greener grass' argument: that if you don't actually have any experience of the private sector, it *might* be better than that of which you do have experience. The possibility of an advantage, however slight, matters more than in some other fields because gains in education affect the whole of the rest of children's lives. Mr H, father of two young children, said he would send them to private school if he could afford it, but qualified his answer. 'Not boarding though, just a day school. I'm not unhappy with state schools – they never did me any harm. But there's a chance that they might be slightly better. You expect a better standard of education if you're paying for it. I know I'm paying for his education out of my taxes, but if you pay directly to the school you think you'd have more say.'

This was a common argument, and was the main reason why those who felt less strongly about standards in state schools said they would go private if they could afford to. It was assumed that private schools had to be better because otherwise why would anyone pay for their children to go to them? Or that paying for something gives you rights to complain about quality – rights that you wouldn't otherwise have (or have the confidence to assert). Or that private schools would have a greater incentive to produce good exam results. It was generally more of an explanation of the obvious than a political manifesto. Mr L of Wolverhampton, father of an 8-year-old boy, said: 'If you could afford it, yes. Well, it teaches them better and more, doesn't it?' His wife disagreed: 'Well, I don't think so. They get a better standard of education at the local schools than at private.' But they agreed, when prompted, that 'if you pay money you've got more say'. Mr L said: 'Yes, because you're paying for it.' Ms L added: 'If you want your value, you're going to speak up, aren't you?'

Ms D, a Conservative with four grown-up children and one 12-year-old, said:

> I would have wanted to send my child to a private school. They give a child a better education in the basics; I think that is lacking in state schools. If you are slow to learn you are left behind in state schools. Whereas with private education that wouldn't be allowed to happen. The school would feel bad if they didn't give good results. [But] I don't feel I would have any more control over my child's education at a private school.

Some of those we asked had never thought of it before. 'I suppose I would have,' said Ms W, an SDP voter in Glasgow with two grown-up daughters. 'I think they've got more time for them and there's not so many in a class. But they were good schools that they went to.'

Some of those who said they would go private were extremely lukewarm. Mr N, SDP, with two children of school age, said: 'If there wasn't a good enough state school or one that wasn't up to the standard that I would want, yes. But it's the same as with the NHS, I can't see any reason why it shouldn't be run just as well as private schools.'

Those who wouldn't, even if they could

The interviews quoted so far, however, do give only one side of the question. The MORI poll quoted at the start of this chapter found that the *other* half of the population would *not* send their children to private school even if they could afford it. It also found that there was a substantial body of support for the comprehensive system as it was (32 per cent). Our interviews suggest that, just as the reasons for supporting private education aren't ideological, the reasons for *not* wanting to send children to private school are not generally to do with an ideological objection to privilege but are immediate and practical. Either people were satisfied with state schools, or people didn't want to send their children away to boarding schools, or private schools were thought to be 'stuck up', isolated from the real world.

'I think our education system is perfectly all right. I don't think you need private schools really,' said Mr D, a 1987 Conservative voter with five children, disagreeing with his wife.

> I suppose if you want to pay for it, fine, but our secondary education system is pretty good. You might get specialised help for your child in a private school if they were having learning difficulties, but you'd have to pay for it. You have to pay for everything in private schools; you don't just pay the fees, you pay for the books and everything. I've never thought my children needed private education. If you're going to be a winner, you'll be a winner wherever you are.

The same view came up in our discussion groups, with Lynn, who said she had voted Conservative 'selfishly', saying: 'I think that if a child has got it, it's got it. You're going to excel anywhere if you're that way inclined. I mean I've been quite happy with the education that my children have had.'

A similar argument was put forward by Ms J, Alliance supporter and mother of three children, although not implying such a hands-off parental approach. 'I believe that if your child is going to do well he'll do well no matter where you send him. I don't think you can put anything into a child's brain that isn't there in the first place. I've been very happy with the state system. I've never worried about the teaching or discipline. All these things start in the home. If you bring them up properly, they'll be okay.'

'I would rather see them grow up. You don't see them except in the school holidays if they're at private school,' said Ms O, Liberal voter in 1987, with two school-age children. Asked whether exam results were important in choosing a school, she said: 'I don't know about exam results. Each child is an individual, and how well they do is up to them. But it's got to have a good reputation. Discipline is important. I don't know how they keep control of some of the classes these days.'

Mr A, unmarried with no children, said:

I personally don't believe in private schools. I don't feel they help children at all. I'm quite happy with state schools. Although I think a child probably would be taught more individually in a private school, I just don't feel a child would appreciate life as he should do. In the state system some schools are badly run. There is a lack of discipline. But more money could improve it. I don't think changing the system will improve matters because that's not where the problem lies. It's lack of teachers and lack of money that's the problem.

Even loyal Labour voters in Glasgow, the only ones of our interviewees to claim a principled objection to private education, advanced only practical arguments. The government would have paid for his children to go to private school, said Mr Y, because he was in the army, 'but I wouldn't do it. The school they went to was a good school. Private education is a kidology. I mean, education needs to be improved. You shouldn't have these kids teaching in schools. Highly qualified men should do it. They should be much more highly qualified with several years of training. But private education is a fallacy.'

Comprehensive versus grammar

Mr K, a Labour-identifying non-voter with two children aged 11 and 15, was lukewarm about private schools. He wouldn't, 'at this point in time', send his children to private school if he could afford it.

But if our state education system got much worse and I had the money, I would say yes. At a private school you would get the best possible tuition and more encouragement for the children so they could achieve their full potential. I am unhappy with the state schools at the moment. I'm not pro the comprehensive system. I believe in comprehensive schooling but with grammar schools brought back. I think they're very necessary in working-class areas for children with ability to succeed. It's the only means for working-class children to achieve if they have the ability. I don't think you can have a blanket comprehensive system that achieves enough for the country. I think different children have different abilities. A large proportion of children are holding back the small proportion of children who could go a lot further.

That desire to have the best of both worlds, the comprehensive and the grammar, is also common. The MORI opinion poll quoted at the start of this chapter was more famous when it was published by *Reader's Digest* in October 1987 for its finding – splashed joyously across the front pages of the Tory press – that '62 per cent of parents want the return of grammar schools'. Of course, they did (and do) want nothing of the sort. MORI's question was exceptionally complicated, and I quote it here in full.[4]

Most state secondary schools in Britain today are comprehensive, which means that children of all abilities attend the same school. Twenty years ago, however, the system was different. There were two types of school – grammar for children who passed an entrance exam known as the Eleven Plus, and secondary modern schools for those who did not.

On this card is a list of possible options which could be adopted in relation to types of state secondary school. Please would you tell me which option most closely describes your view.

Go back to grammar and secondary modern schools, with entrance to grammar school being determined by an exam pass mark.	17 per cent
Go back to grammar and secondary modern schools, with entrance to grammar schools being determined by continuous assessment rather than an exam pass mark.	45 per cent
Keep the present system of having comprehensive schools in Britain.	32 per cent
Don't know.	6 per cent

The Tory press added together the first two figures to produce their majority for 'a return to the grammar school system'. But what the poll really showed was, in a sense, the opposite of what they claimed: it revealed the extent of the hostility to the divisive Eleven Plus exam which used to condemn four out of every five children (and a much higher proportion of working-class children) to a second-class education, restricting their opportunities for life.[5] What the poll also shows, however, is a strong feeling that the comprehensive system has not worked well. What people want is grammar schools without the Eleven Plus – the quality of grammar school education for all. (Whether all MORI's respondents knew what 'continuous assessment' was is doubtful: what they may have deduced was that it wasn't the Eleven Plus.)

Attitudes to grammar schools are similar to the aspiration to private education. What many people want is 'schools as good as private schools (are assumed to be)' for all. Of course, that may not be what they really want: what they may *really* want is a school as good as a private or grammar school for *their* child. But they realise that the best way of guaranteeing that – assuming that they can't in fact afford it – is to seek as extensive and open provision as possible. This is why comprehensive schools were popular when they were introduced in the 1960s. Working-class parents were not all committed to equality as a principle, but many of them recognised that an egalitarian education policy would give their children a better chance than a system divided by a class-loaded selection process.

This is also why comprehensives became unpopular in the 1970s and 1980s. Ms M, a retired primary school teacher in Wolverhampton, put it most bitterly: 'Comprehensive schools have been a disaster; they have betrayed working-class children.' It became clear that abolishing the hated Eleven Plus and integrating schools had not significantly opened up the higher reaches of educational attainment to working-class children. Hence Mr K's reference right back to an even earlier stage of the education debate, the time when grammar schools were seen as the pro-working-class solution to the divisiveness of an education system dominated by the privilege of precisely the 'English public schools' that Gallup found to be more unpopular in the 1960s than simple 'private schools' are now. Like comprehensives, grammar schools initially promised the working classes much and ended by delivering disappointment. They were seen as offering an avenue to higher education that was open to all children on the basis of ability and regardless of class. For many working-class children grammar schools did indeed provide this avenue, but it gradually became clear that (a) there was a strong class bias in the measuring of 'ability', and (b) the chances were remote of recovering from failure in the selection exam at the arbitrary age of eleven. What many people wanted when they supported comprehensives was not so much egalitarianism as a fairer meritocracy.

Opting out

The alternative strategy to providing the quality of grammar or private school education for all is simply to opt out of the state system. To do so individually is expensive, hence the Conservative measure to allow whole schools to opt out while still being funded by the taxpayer. Gould Mattinson's post-election interviews found that awareness of the specifics of Conservative policy was fairly low, although those who were more aware mentioned the idea of 'giving parents more say' and taking power away from local councils, and a few mentioned opting out. Where Labour defectors were aware of these policies, they were positive about them because they will mean 'more choice'. 'Parents should be able to choose where they send their kids – it's their right.' 'It's the best way to make sure bright kids don't get held back – that's what happens when they all get sent to the same school.' 'It'll stop the extremists getting their way.' Paying for extras in the state system was seen as a 'rip off', and even schools opting out of local council control was often not enough to satisfy the desire for private education.

Only one of our interviewees mentioned the Conservative plans, when asked whether he would have more say over what was taught if his children were at a private school: 'Yes, possibly. Although there's new legislation so that, as long as you're interested and go along to the board meetings, you can make your views known' (Mr N, Wolverhampton SDP voter).

Opinion polls show that opting out was unpopular at the 1987 election, and continued to be so. A Marplan poll for *The Guardian*, with an anti-government bias in the question, found only 18 per cent in favour of schools in their area opting out, 61 per cent wanted them to remain, and 21 per cent didn't know or weren't sure, in January 1988. But even a MORI poll, with a pro-government bias in the question, could only drum up 34 per cent in favour of opting out, with 43 per cent against, in December

1987. Marplan asked if people favoured schools in their area opting out of local council control to 'be funded directly from central government'. MORI asked if people favoured schools being 'given the power to opt out of local council control. In the Marplan poll, parents with children currently at school were more strongly opposed than the rest.

Some Labour and Alliance voters interviewed by Gould Mattinson, mainly middle-class or clerical workers, specifically attacked the Tory concept of 'choice;: If they spent more on state schools so they were really decent, the whole idea of choice would be irrelevant.' 'What "choice" means is that rich people get a good deal at everyone else's expense.' 'You can't talk about choice when it's only open to the top few per cent of the population.'

But among Conservative converts, Labour's hostility to private education was interpreted as hostility to the very possibility of choice. A large majority of all voters felt that Labour would improve state education, although awareness of what Labour would actually do was low, with many people saying that they hadn't a clue. Among those with an opinion, the main assumption was that Labour would spend more money, which a majority of all but convinced Tories felt was a good thing. 'There'd be more of everything to go round.' 'They'd pay teachers more, which would mean a much better standard of teaching.' 'They'd give more people a chance of further education.' The fact that awareness of specific policies was low meant that some believed (incorrectly) that Labour wanted to abolish private schools. 'They'd make everyone go to the same type of school – there'd be no choice.' 'They'd want everyone to be the same – you might want the best for your children, but that's tough.' 'Why shouldn't you pay for a good school if you've got the money?'

In our interviews, we asked 'Are there too many permissive or trendy subjects being taught in schools?' as an open-ended question. This was almost always accepted as code for teaching about (or just 'teaching') sex and homosexuality. Discussion of homosexuality in schools was widely disapproved of, but sometimes only because it was believed to have 'gone too far'. In many cases people admitted that they had no experience of the issue at their children's school. 'That's my impression,' said Mr N, 'but it's only really known from the media.'

The press campaign against some Labour local councils during 1986 exploited prejudice against ethnic minorities and homosexuals through society's most vulnerable point of attack, its children. The spectre of threats to children was used to mobilise prejudice even among those not used to thinking of themselves as prejudiced. British Social Attitudes surveys show that many more white people would object to their children marrying an Asian or black person (51 per cent) than admit to being prejudiced against ethnic minorities (36 per cent). More people also think that homosexuals should not be allowed to adopt children (93 per cent, according to Gallup) than admit to thinking homosexuality is always or mostly wrong (74 per cent).[7]

It is no coincidence that in 1986 the focus of attack for the Tory tabloids switched from Labour councils like Lambeth, Hackney and Islington, which are in inner London and were therefore not education authorities (being under the then Inner London Education Authority), to boroughs like Brent and Haringey, which are outside ILEA and are education authorities. The Maureen McGoldrick affair in Brent (where a head teacher was unfairly accused of racism) and an inept 'positive images of homosexuality' policy in Haringey provided the tabloids with a core of real material around which they could create a suggestive tableau inhabited by phantasms of the popular imagination.

Mr H, Basildon father of two, asked if too many trendy subjects were being taught in schools, said:

> Not at my son's school. But you hear on the news about schools where they do teach about homosexuality and I think that is wrong. There's nothing wrong with sex education when they're old enough to understand, but not gay rights. Then you hear about nursery rhymes being banned because they are supposedly racist. We're not racist round here. We don't hide anything from him – if he asks we tell him. He knows he can come to us with any sort of question.

Mr K, another Basildon father of two, said:

> Probably, but I don't have a bee in my bonnet about it. I'm not a gay rights supporter but nor am I of a belief in authoritarianism against gay people. I don't believe it should be

encouraged in some schools in London as much as it is. Some people may waver between homosexuality and heterosexuality and they can be encouraged to become gay. I don't think it's good for them or society if too many people are encouraged along those lines.

According to Mr D, Putney father of five, 'there is a time and place for teaching children about homosexuality. I think you should wait until they're older; 11 and 12 is too young. They don't need to know all about that, and I don't think they're particularly interested anyway.' And Ms J, Basildon parent, said: 'My children probably know more about gays than I do. The way society is today, they probably know a lot about homosexuality. I don't think it should be taught in schools.'

Mr A, a Putney non-parent:

I think they've gone too far in teaching about the gay movement. I don't think it's really a subject that needs to be taught to people at school. As they grow older they know full well what their tendencies are, they don't need to have it drummed into them one way or the other while they are at school. It's a waste of time and they should be taught useful things. Sex education should be taught because with things like Aids around they haven't really got an awful lot of choice.

Lastly Ms C, one of the pensioners among whom the lesbian and gay rights issue was 'costing us dear', according to Labour leader Neil Kinnock's press secretary, felt that 'all this talk about gay rights makes children inquisitive. Livingstone and Labour are pushing that issue far too much. There always have been gays, but he wants to keep bringing it up and pushing it as though that is the way things should be.' Her husband agreed. 'It should be left as it was before, kept under cover.'

These issues may have more power to influence people's voting decisions, by tapping great reservoirs of irrational feeling, than any supposed shift in values that are more conventionally thought of as political – from left to right, or from collectivist to individualist. Education is a good example of where an apparent increase in support for private provision, which appears to be based in the sphere of economics (the 'free' market versus the state), really arises in the social sphere (attitudes to sex and race). This would seem to challenge Anthony Heath and Richard Topf's conclusion (in their essay on 'Political Culture', *British Social Attitudes: The 1987 Report*) that British political culture 'connects *economic* and political values much more than it connects *moral* and political values'. The links between individualism and sexual and racial prejudice are examined further, in Chapter 10.

However, by no means all voters are susceptible to such influences. Ms D, a Thatcherite on economics in the last chapter, and who would have sent her child to a private school if she could have afforded it, said: 'My son is learning about various religions at the moment and I think that's rather nice. Children shouldn't just be taught about Christianity. [And] on sex education, I hope they'll teach him that there is nothing wrong in being gay – there's nothing harmful.' And Ms E, an Alliance voter with four grown-up children, said: 'Christian teaching is very important. I'm a Christian and I would want my religion to be passed onto my children. To teach sex at primary level is nonsense; there's no need for it and the time would be better spent on the three Rs.' But she added: 'It's very essential that race awareness is taught. We should be able to get on with our fellow men.'

Summary

Although many people say they would send their children to a private school if they could afford it, this does not mean that they think that education generally should be provided privately. Only one in ten people who didn't themselves go to private schools believe the private sector should be expanded, according to British Society Attitudes surveys. The 13 per cent of the adult population who have attended a British private school at some time or other are nearly twice as keen to see more private provision, but it is rare for people who have not been privately educated to want more private schools.[8] The aspiration to private education does not mean that people actually think that private provision for everybody is a good idea.

According to some commentators, private education represents the pinnacle of enterprise and opportunity for new working-class

Conservatives in the South. A few enthusiastic converts may see it in these terms, but most aspire to it in the same way that, if they had the money, they would buy a Rolls-Royce because it is a better car. Gould Mattinson interviewed one C1 woman who said 'Labour policy has meant over-achievers were slowed down, but it's not going to alter for me as my children go private,' but she is hardly typical. Most have little idea of the actual costs, but believe that it may be affordable in the future, possibly through an insurance or savings scheme as with private health care. 'I've seen these ads in the paper where you put so much by a month – we thought we might go for that.'

In general, people want the best possible education for their children and are ideologically indifferent as to how to achieve it. Where the politics come in is in what people think of as being the best. Private and grammar schools provide the models for everything desirable in education because they are the routes to advancement for the privileged, so they are bound to be models which carry strong class overtones.

Idealised notions of private schools are often not based on experience, however. Several times our interviewees make judgements about private schools based on assumptions about what they 'would be' or are 'probably' like. When BBC2's *Forty Minutes* 'Changing Places' (11 February 1988) featured two groups of sixth-formers from a comprehensive school in Kirkby, Merseyside, and Rugby, the Midlands private school, who changed places for a week, one Kirkby schoolgirl commented: 'You know, a lot of people say "If I had the money I'd send my children to public school", but after this week I'd never. I'd never send my children to public school. I'd kill myself.'

It is not just the ideals of private and grammar schools that are cultural constructs, distanced from reality. Ideas about educational standards are indicative of a society's dreams and fears. The 'three Rs' are repeatedly intoned as if they were a magic formula.[9] Frequent references to the 'three Rs', and to 'the basics', thought to be much neglected, indicate attitudes towards education that often start from experience, but which take on an independent life of their own. They are associated with the idea of a society in decline.

One of Gould Mattinson's conclusions from their post-election research in 1987 was that ex-Labour voters were more likely to see education as a chance to 'better yourself'. 'The difference is what you do for yourself – it doesn't matter what background you come from. The facilities are there for your education – there's night schools – you can better yourself' (C1 Conservative woman). 'More people go to university. I shall boot my kids all the way up the ladder' (West Midlands C1 Conservative man). 'You've got to look at it as forward planning. We're all trying to better ourselves, trying to make as much money as we can' (C1 Conservative woman).

It is this aspiration to better themselves which is important in the politics of individualism, not the specific desire for private provision which sometimes accompanies it. Labour has lost ground to the Conservatives in the last three elections, not because that ground has shifted under the party's feet but because Labour has failed to hold on to and renew its support among those, the non-manual working class especially, who are ambitious for themselves and their families. There may not have been an increase in individualism, but the more individualistic of Labour's supporters may have defected to the centre parties or the Conservatives.

4

Housing

I'm the first generation of my family to own a house and the wife is the first generation of her family to own – that's a step in the right direction.

The selling of council houses is claimed by the Conservatives, and conceded by many of their enemies, to have been one of their most successful policies. Since 1979, 1.1 million homes have been sold at an average discount of nearly 50 per cent. Sales peaked in 1982, and in January 1987 the government introduced new measures to keep up the momentum, increasing the cash limit on the value of discounts from £25,000 to £35,000 and the maximum discount on flats to 70 per cent.

Under Mrs Thatcher the proportion of UK homes that are owner-occupied has risen from 56 per cent to 63 per cent, and three-quarters of that increase is because of council house sales. Not surprisingly, the policy of selling council houses is popular with those council tenants who can afford to buy. A donation of £35,000 with no strings attached is not likely to induce hostility towards the donor. 'If I was in that situation I would buy – it's like giving people money on a plate,' said a Don't Know interviewed by Gould Mattinson. But there are three other important questions: Do council house sales actually make people vote Tory? Are they popular with people who don't benefit? And does the spread of home ownership mean that people are more selfish or self-reliant than they used to be? The answers are no, no and no.

Home ownership is, and has been for decades, more desirable than renting in Britain. But this is mainly because of its strong financial advantages. And the reasons for the spread of home ownership are mostly financial as well. Steadily rising living standards

53

mean more and more people can afford to buy. Home ownership is neither a symptom nor a cause of 'individualist' attitudes. People do not buy their own home because they believe it is wrong to depend on the state to provide a place to live; nor do people who have bought their home adopt different attitudes towards public and private provision. On the contrary, most people who buy their council home believe strongly that the state, local or national, should provide housing for those who can't afford to buy. People simply do not think what the government wants them to think.

More specifically, buying your council home has little or no direct effect on voting behaviour. And, more generally, home ownership has little effect on voting – once people's social class is taken into account. If home owners, private renters and council tenants had voted the same way in 1983 as they did in 1964, then the rise of home ownership would have increased the Conservative vote by just 1.5 percentage points and reduced the Labour vote by the same amount, if everything else, including the size of the various social classes, had stayed the same.[1]

But let us examine those three questions one by one.

Do council house sales win votes for the Tories?

It seems obvious that they do. Certainly the Conservatives think so, although Margaret Thatcher still feels she has to exaggerate the extent of home ownership: 'Today, two out of three families own their own homes.' (It was 61 per cent.) And she seemed to believe not so much that sales could win votes for the Conservative Party, but that they could lose votes for Labour: 'A million people would not own the home they do if the Tories had not introduced the Right to Buy. Would Labour let you keep your newly bought council house? You know that they didn't want you to have it. Given half a chance, they'd take it away from you. And they certainly wouldn't be keen on other names being added to the list of owners' (9 June 1987).

Local Conservative Associations have set up Right-to-Buy clubs which encourage council tenants to buy their homes and try to associate their right to do so with Toryism. In Haringey in north London, for example, councillor Peter Murphy writes frequently to tenants who have applied to buy. As a politician he acts as a financial adviser and estate agent; as the Right-to-Buy Club he offers dispassionate advice on politics. On Tottenham Conservative Association headed paper he has written to tenants: 'We are also able to give you advice as to financing, the right sort of solicitor to use, whether to appeal and matters like that. In any event please do not hesitate to call in and see us and hopefully you will very shortly be the owner of your home.' Meanwhile, on 'Right-to-Buy Club' headed paper he wrote in May 1987: 'In the unhappy event of the Conservative government failing to win the election I hold out no prospect for you buying your property from Haringey council. For this reason it would not seem sensible to vote Labour but that is a matter for your individual decision.'

The Labour Party also thinks council house sales win Tory votes, and it has overcome its early opposition to the Right to Buy, although not very enthusiastically. In Scotland, where only 40 per cent of homes are owner-occupied, several Labour supporters I interviewed still saw home ownership as a threat. 'People are so selfish,' said a solicitor. 'They think because they have a little semi that they've got it all. Just because they've got a tiny bit they vote for the government that gave it to them. People are so stupid and small-minded. They come home and watch television and the rest of the world can go to hell.'

Ms V, a widow and a homeowner herself, commented more temperately: 'There are all these people buying houses – they're not better off because they've got to pay the mortgage, but they feel they ought to vote Tory, just because they've got their own house.'

The hopes of the Conservative Party and the fears of Labour supporters are not evidence enough that selling council houses is the same as buying votes. Much more convincing evidence, however, is presented by council house purchasers themselves. After its disastrous General Election results in the capital, the London Labour Party conducted an inquiry into why a popular local MP, Alf Dubs, lost his seat in Battersea. Discussions with small groups of ex-Labour voters confirmed that the euphemistically named 'London Effect' was still echoing through their political consciousness – hostility to the lesbian and gay rights policies of some London Labour councils does exist. But far more important, it appears, was the effect of the Right to Buy. One voter said:

'It wasn't a foregone conclusion with me. It was a fact that Wandsworth borough who are a Conservative borough gave me indirectly £50,000 so I voted for them.' Another, asked her reasons for not voting Labour, said:

> Personal gain for me, really, because if Labour got in they could have scrubbed the Right to Buy, and that would have knocked me straight out and also my kids – there is a second-generation purchasing power within the Right to Buy and I was after them, getting them to buy flats – as they become vacant – through the council. This is all by the Conservatives and if Labour got in they could have knocked it on the head.

According to Deborah Mattinson, commenting on Gould Mattinson's post-election research, home ownership is the single most important symbol of the changed circumstances of the new affluent Conservative voter. Direct political gratitude was often expressed by council house buyers: 'She's given me the opportunity to buy – nobody in my family has ever had that chance before' (C2 Conservative woman).

Our own group discussions for this book reinforced this message. They were conducted in Roehampton, further out than Battersea, but still in Wandsworth borough, and so still experiencing the full weight of the 'Right to Buy Effect'. Jonathan, a 'soft' Tory, said: 'One of the best things that the Conservatives ever did was the home ownership situation. It's the only good thing she ever did for me, she got me my house.'

Lynn, a Conservative voter in 1983 and 1987, said: 'Basically I voted selfishly because I think that if the Labour got in, in this particular area, they don't want you to buy your property, so they would make it harder.' (Although when she was asked if Labour's threat to home ownership was the only reason she voted Tory, she retreated a little, saying: 'I'm not really for any of them.')

Ann, who said she had switched to the Tories in 1987, was more categorical: 'We voted Conservative purely because we're buying our own home, and my daughter is buying her home. And we thought that if Labour got in, I mean at our ages, we don't stand a chance of buying private, so this was the big chance for us.'

One of the prejudices informing this book is that what people say about their motives should be believed rather than interpreted through condescending assumptions about what they 'really' want. If people say they changed their vote because they bought their council house, then I believe them.

Nevertheless, what 'some people say' is not evidence for the attitudes and values of a whole nation. What our interviewees say is important, but should be used only to broaden our understanding of the evidence of scientific surveys. The evidence of opinion polls must come first, and on the question of council house sales it is quite startling. It shows that people who have bought their council house are no more likely to vote Conservative after buying than they were before. This was first discovered by Heath, Jowell and Curtice, the best debunkers in political analysis, in their survey of the 1983 General Election (*How Britain Votes*, pp. 49–51). They showed that 23 per cent of council tenants voted Conservative in 1983, and exactly the same percentage said they had voted Conservative in 1979. Of those ex-council tenants who had bought their homes, 40 per cent voted Conservative in 1983 – but exactly the same percentage said they had voted Tory in 1979. So, although council house purchasers are more Conservative than those they leave behind in the public sector, they were more Conservative in the first place. Clearly, those who can afford to buy are better off – they are not on the dole, for instance – and hence more likely to vote Conservative anyway.

The number of people in Heath, Jowell and Curtice's sample of council house buyers was very small by opinion poll standards (126). But the finding is backed up by the apparent absence of a similar effect on people who bought, and profited from, privatisation share issues (see p. 100). The amounts of cash involved are smaller, but the principle is the same. It is of course true that 'you cannot prove a negative', but it *can* be said that if there is an effect it cannot be very great. (There is, for example, the proven tendency of people to mis-remember their past voting behaviour in order to bring it in line with their present party loyalty. So, some of the council house purchasers who voted Tory in 1983 could have 'forgotten' that they had switched since the previous election.) And any effect there might be operates on a relatively small section of the total population.

So what is to be made of the comments of lapsed Labour voters in Battersea? It is possible that the people expressing forceful pro-Tory views – the ones that stand out in the transcripts of group discussions – may not be typical of council house buyers in general. In Wolverhampton I interviewed Mr S, who had bought his council house six months before the 1987 election, in which he switched *back* to Labour from the SDP. 'Owning the house' was his biggest achievement in life, but he saw no connection between that and how he voted.

Deborah Mattinson describes home ownership as an important 'symbol' of changed personal circumstances; it does not *cause* Conservative support, but it is identified with it and so is stressed, especially by new converts, as a kind of badge of their affiliation. Another man in Wolverhampton, Mr R, a metal mechanic who had bought his (not ex-council) house, emphatically identified his Tory loyalty with home ownership, banging his front door to make his point. But he had always voted Tory, 'except when I'd just left school and before I knew better', when he voted Labour once. *His* main political concern, far from being home ownership, was with the country being too overcrowded, 'because there are so many immigrants, which we don't want'.

Margaret Thatcher's 1987 election campaign speech, quoted on p. 54, is also revealing: council house sales may not have been a vote winner, but the widespread misunderstanding of Labour's position, and the party's complete inability to convey a positive message to homeowners, certainly did not provide an incentive to vote Labour. There is a difference: it wasn't that the Conservatives had recruited people to new values of individualism, it was that Labour had allowed itself to become trapped in a caricature which appeared to threaten what people had already gained and to obstruct those who hoped to benefit.

Bryan Gould commented candidly on Labour's early opposition to the Right to Buy during the party's post-election policy review. 'The sort of apartheid that we object to in education and the health service on socialist grounds we supported in housing. It was crazy. We said to people: "You are tenants and by god that's how you'll stay" ' (Tower Hamlets Fabian Society, 13 April 1988).

Of course it is possible that Battersea isn't typical. In the borough of Wandsworth an unusually ideological Conservative council had sold 9,000 homes in eight years by 1986 in a high-profile campaign. If working-class voters were defecting from Labour to the Conservatives because of London's prosperity (which they were, Chapter 9), then they would be more likely in Wandsworth than most places to seize on council house sales as an example of the link between their prosperity and the Conservative Party. In addition, house prices in London are higher and have risen faster than elsewhere in the country, making the size of the inducement often spectacular, as the person who referred to his gain of £50,000 confirms. If there is a slight council house sales effect, Wandsworth is the one part of the country where it would be felt.

Are council house sales popular among people who don't benefit from them?

The answer to this question also seems obvious. Gallup's big survey during the 1979 General Election found that 74 per cent of the population thought 'selling more council houses to tenants' was a good idea, and just 19 per cent opposed it. But the idea that this is a recent enthusiasm is quite wrong. Another Gallup poll, carried out as long ago as 1967, found that exactly the same proportion approved of 'local authorities [being] willing to sell council houses to the occupiers'. Seventeen per cent disapproved.

Furthermore, this support may be wide, but it is not deep. If it is examined in more depth, it seems that people are mostly expressing tolerance of what other people get up to, a general principle that people should be allowed to do things unless there are compelling reasons why not. They realise that selling council houses makes it harder to house people in need, but that is not the fault of the individual house purchaser. Most of the people we interviewed were or had been council tenants, and almost all of them said 'Yes' when asked if council house sales were a good idea, but many heavily qualified their response. 'It gives more people the opportunity to buy a house, but it also cuts down on the amount of flats and houses available for people who can't afford it. In many ways – I know that the council house waiting list is increasing all the time – I disagree with selling them off' (Mr B, Putney skilled worker). 'If we were younger we would have definitely bought this flat. In a way the sales are a good idea. But you do stop people, especially youngsters, from getting a place to live. She's just not building any new homes' (Mr C, Putney pensioner). 'It was good in our case. But I don't think the sales are good for the younger generation. My children haven't got a hope in hell of getting a council place. There's good and bad to the policy' (Ms J, Basildon Alliance supporter).

Given that owning your home is overwhelmingly thought of as a desirable thing, people are perhaps reluctant to penalise individuals for the sake of a collective benefit in the future, or to penalise them for central government's obstruction of new house building.

The British Social Attitudes surveys recognise that views on council house sales cannot be reduced to a yes–no answer to a straight question. In 1985, it offered three statements: 'Council tenants should not be allowed to buy their houses or flats'; 'Council tenants should be allowed to buy but only in areas with no housing shortage'; and 'Council tenants should generally be allowed to buy their houses or flats'. Compared with Gallup's 1979 survey, unconditional support for sales was reduced from 74 to 60 per cent. Outright opposition to sales was halved from 19 to 9 per cent, while 29 per cent opted for the conditional statement (*British Social Attitudes: The 1986 Report*, p. 241). The phrase 'housing shortage' provides a rationale for curtailing individual rights in the name of 'shared austerity', a principle that also crops up in attitudes to the health service. This is not enough for the 60 per cent who prefer unrestricted sales, but that doesn't mean that they are blind to the drawbacks.

A policy which backed the Right to Buy with new council building would clearly be much more popular than either the present Conservative policy or a 'Labour fundamentalist' policy of concentrating on new council building to the exclusion of all other forms of housing (such as that pursued by the Militant-tendency dominated Labour council in Liverpool 1983–6).

I don't think council house sales are a good idea. I'd agree with it if they were replaced, but they don't seem to be doing that at the moment. If they could replace them as quickly as they sell them then that would be great, it would give more people a chance to own. The young, elderly and those who can't afford to buy will always need council housing. Not everybody can afford their own home. There will always be the unemployed, although there's not as many as there once were.

Mr H, a Basildon home-owner (not bought from council), and a Conservative who last voted Labour in 1979, continued: 'It's the responsibility of both the government and local councils to provide housing. We put them into power for our benefit and they should be providing people with some form of shelter. It's disgusting that people have to stay in bed and breakfast. I've seen it on the telly, a young mum with three kids in a room not the size of our living-room.'

The fact that he blamed the government and not the 'young mum' is particularly interesting in the light of common attitudes to social security scroungers (see Chapter 8). He is a particularly clear example of someone whose willingness to vote Conservative does not imply an acceptance of Tory values.

Several of the participants in our group discussions, beneficiaries of the Right to Buy, were critical of the government's 'Wrong to Replace' policy. Jane, a Tory voter in 1983 and 1987, but now beginning to regret it, said: 'I think they [the Conservatives] have given people the opportunity to buy their own places, but while people are buying them they're not building, so they're not providing for people who can't afford to buy.'

David, a hard-line Tory but a council housing officer, said that the trouble with council house sales is 'they're not replenishing what they sell. And that is what I object to.' Others of the group agreed. Jonathan: 'It does seem terribly hard for young people to get housing now, I don't know how they do it. I don't know that they think about youngsters.' Tony: 'They're not getting any great discount when they buy the council property, are they, the youngsters? You need to be a council tenant for years and you get a decent refund. And they've got to take on £40,000 or £50,000 mortgages.'

The possible obstacles to support for a policy of 'Right to Buy plus new building' might be hostility towards public spending or a lack of faith in the ability of councils to manage housing efficiently, but neither of these troubled our interviewees.

Housing is overwhelmingly seen as a government responsibility; it is also a high priority, coming third after the health service and education as people's choice for extra public spending, and last or next-to-last choice for spending cuts (Gallup, August and December 1987). Gould Mattinson's post-election survey shows that *this* support – unlike support for council house sales – is not hedged about with many qualifications. One C2 Conservative, comparing Labour and Tory policies on housing, mentioned cost: 'I think the Labour Party would build more, which we should do, but the cost would hit everyone.' But there was general recognition of the limits to individualism when it comes to providing a roof over people's heads. 'They [the government] should provide housing because people can't afford to get it otherwise' (C2 Conservative). 'The government has a duty to provide housing' (Ex-Labour, non-voter). 'More building needs to be done, otherwise the rich will become richer and the poor poorer' (C1 Conservative). One C1 woman who voted Conservative echoed Mr H's strikingly anti-Thatcherite sentiments on homelessness: 'It's a scandal, all these children in bed-and-breakfasts – the government should do something about it.'

There are indeed limits to council house sales – the average cost of a council home after discount in 1986/87 was still £14,500. Mrs Thatcher has said that her target is for three-quarters of all homes to be owner-occupied, but at this rate it will take until the year 2005, and the building societies say already that the market for home ownership is 'saturated': those that don't own can't afford houses almost at any price, no matter how big a discount the government forces local councils to give.

As Ms E, a Putney home owner who voted Alliance in 1987, said: 'It isn't possible for everybody to own their own home: those at the lower end of the scale just can't afford it, and we must provide for them for a stable society. I think for those who can afford to buy the council house sales are a good idea. But we still have to provide homes for people instead of putting them into hotels.'

Only a very small minority of Gould Mattinson's ex-Labour voters expressed a pure individualist position, and said that the government shouldn't provide housing at all, or only for the very needy poor. 'It's not the government's responsibility. Everyone's responsible for themselves, no one should provide for anyone' (C2 Conservative). 'The government wants people to have their own responsibility and not come begging to the state for what they want – we need self-reliance' (C1 Conservative).

But a perhaps even smaller minority ought also to be noted, who expressed a pure collectivist position, such as Ms O, whom I interviewed in Wolverhampton, a Labour-to-Liberal defector in

1987 who lived in a council house and 'can't afford' to buy it. 'I don't think council house sales are a good idea. We managed before. Everybody did without [them]. Everybody managed in council houses before.'

Far more common was the view which combined an 'individualist' preference for home ownership with a 'collectivist' desire for the government or local councils to provide properly for those who couldn't afford it. Mr A, a council tenant in Putney who thought of himself as Labour despite having voted Alliance in 1987, stressed the need for a higher standard of public housing. 'I think the government should take on more of the responsibility because they've cut the local councils' expenditure so much that they just haven't got the money or the places for the homeless. They should build good-quality housing and not put people into the dumps where many people live now. I'm happy living on this council estate, although it would be better to live in a house.'

This concern with the quality of public housing was frequently repeated, but is not particularly related to party-political views of how housing should be provided. It appears not to reflect a belief that local councils are inherently inefficient in building and housing management, because it often contains the assumption that more money, and a bit more care and attention, would put the problem right. Mr D, another Putney council tenant, who voted Conservative for the first time in 1987, said: 'Either the government or councils should provide housing because that is one of life's basic needs. Ideally everyone who needs a home should be provided with one. Housing should be of good quality. They've learnt their mistakes from the 1960s and realised you can't just cram people into tower blocks.'

Mr H, the Conservative Basildon home owner who thought it was 'disgusting' that people have to stay in bed-and-breakfast accommodation, said: 'Everyone should be able to get council housing. We lived in a council flat for three years, it was a bit of a hole but a lick of paint put it to rights. They've made lots of mistakes in the past, with flats falling down, and they should take a lot more time and trouble to provide good housing in the future.'

Ms J, an Alliance supporter who bought her house from Basildon council five years ago after being a council tenant for fourteen years, agreed that the council had a responsibility to house people, but 'it should be properly built homes, not put up in an afternoon. We lived in a prefab for nine months and it was terrible. It fell to pieces eventually. One of the reasons we came out here was because we were only offered a flat in a tower block back in Poplar. I turned down Ronan Point, the tower block that eventually fell down.'

These opinions, all expressed by ex-Labour voters, are some way off a new Thatcherite individualism, a desire to see others showing more self-reliance. They could be dismissed as pious statements of charitable intent – the poor should be provided for – if it weren't for the fact that they reflect support for people *like themselves* having access through collective council housing to the individual goal of home ownership. Ms J went on to say: 'They [the council] should help the people who can't afford to buy. The people who need a foothold on the first rung of the ladder towards buying. There are a lot of couples, both working, who can afford to buy and they should be encouraged to do so. But the others should be given a chance by the council.'

So public housing is seen as a good thing on two grounds: it provides for the deserving poor, and it enables others who are not rich to achieve the even more desirable goal of home ownership.

Is the popularity of home ownership a sign of greater individualism?

Two related fallacies underlie this one. One is the confusion of 'giving people money on a plate' with winning support for an ideology. The other is the confusion of the desirability of home ownership with individualism, and hence the spread of home ownership with the spread of individualism.

There are 'individualist' advantages of home ownership: 'It makes people feel independent – you can choose your own neighbours' (Mr N); 'We can now do what we like to it' (Ms J); 'It gives you pride and security' (Ms E); 'You're more in charge of your destiny' (Ms D). But these advantages are much easier to appreciate while they are so heavily subsidised by the taxpayer. Might not attitudes to owning as opposed to renting be different if the £4 billion a year of tax relief were switched from owner-occupation to renting? If you could set your rent against income tax instead of mortgage payments, and if capital gains on houses were taxed, some people might well wax lyrical about the 'independence' of the private rented sector or the 'security' of council housing. Attitudes to owning and renting are certainly different in other countries, because the structures of public subsidy are different. (That might raise the question of why Britain went down the road of subsidised mass owner-occupation in the first place, but the answer to that lies a long way back in the country's history, and not in any supposed rise of individualism in the 1980s.)

Most of our interviewees, indeed, stressed the financial advantages of owning as much as the independence. 'It's nice not to have to pay rent every week to the council. It's nice to have your own place and know full well that, if you do look after it, the price of the house will rise, you'll be able to sell it and make some money on it. Financially, it's much better to own,' said Mr A, a Putney council tenant.

Among those who had actually bought, the financial advantages were associated with a great sense of achievement. 'I'm the first generation of my family to own a house and the wife is the first generation of her family to own – that's a step in the right direction. It gives us security. And I was always taught that you can't go wrong with bricks and mortar. The house has doubled its price in three years, which is pretty good,' said Mr H, Basildon home owner (not bought from the council), who last voted Labour in 1979.

Ms J, who had bought her house from Basildon council five years before, also saw home ownership as a great step forward for the family. She is an Alliance supporter who last voted Labour in 1966 ('I could see myself voting Labour again if they went back to what the old Labour Party stood for – I have very fond memories of the Wilson years').

I'm pleased that we've bought this house. We've bashed out walls and windows and got it to how we like it. With the council you don't have the same motivation. You feel as if you're making the improvements for somebody else and not yourself.

For us, it was a good investment because of the discount. We'll now be able to move wherever we want to. I don't think it's a good idea for everybody to own. It could take some people out of their depth. I think when they get to the bottom of what's involved and how much the upkeep costs, many people change their minds. It was a much bigger financial commitment for ourselves to go from paying rent to buying, it was a hell of a shock.

At the time, my husband was very reluctant to buy. He wondered if we could afford it. I really had to push for it. We're the first generation in both our families to own our own home. My father is still in a council flat. But my husband's parents have since bought their council house and his two sisters have bought and my two brothers have bought their council houses.

Similar, although more ambivalent, sentiments were also expressed by Mr D, despite being in a quite different position: a Putney Conservative voter who *hadn't* bought his council house.

If you own your own home it gives you roots which is very important, especially if you have a family. I'm not so sure that it gives you a sense of security: if you can't keep up with the repayments you lose your house. [And] I don't think it's a question of independence. You can do what you like to a council house, as long as you improve it. Generally, it is better for people to own their own homes. Everyone should have the chance of owning their own home; whether everyone can or not, I don't know. [But] I don't think it's necessarily essential. I've never owned my own home and it's never really bothered me. I don't feel like a second-class citizen because I don't own this. And, anyway, if you're taking out a mortgage you don't own the house until you've paid your mortgage off.

Gould Mattinson found themes of responsibility and self-reliance in the self-image of ex-Labour voters that were associated with home ownership: 'It's good to own your own house and take responsibility – do your own repairs and release money for the council to do something else'. But they also found the same themes among Tory council tenants: 'If anything needs to be done [in my council flat] I do it myself. A Labour person would probably wait for the council to come and do it'.

Summary

Home ownership is more desirable than renting in Britain, mostly for financial reasons. In return for high – but subsidised – mortgage costs home owners accumulate capital assets and roll up tax-free capital gains as house prices rise faster than inflation over the years. The long-term trend towards greater home ownership is the result of rising real earnings for most of those in employment, which enables more and more people to afford these advantages.

The acceleration of this trend in the 1980s is the product of another financial incentive: the discounts on council house sales. But buying a council home has little or no direct effect on how people vote, or on their political attitudes.

Of course, as (most) people get richer, the need to provide housing collectively for the less well off slowly diminishes. And owning property may, over time, change a family's political outlook, although the evidence suggests that class (determined by occupation) is much more important. The growth of the (home owning) middle class and the shrinking of the (council renting) working class clearly has long-term implications for the Labour Party. But it is the class changes, not the tenure changes, that matter. Those implications would be terminal if the middle class were in some profound way more 'individualist' than the working class. But it could be that the middle class are only more individualist in that they are more likely to be able to afford to opt out of collective housing, health care and education. Do middle-class and working-class people actually want different things, regardless of what they can afford? The answer given in this chapter is emphatically 'No'. Working-class people are more likely to favour a collective effort to provide housing for everyone because it is often the only way they can achieve the same goal of home ownership.

Our interviews reveal that even among those who have switched their vote from Labour to Conservative there is strong support for state provision of housing at the same time as for council house sales. Although glad to benefit, several council house buyers expressed worries that sales stored up longer-term problems. Two working-class Conservative women interviewed by Gould Mattinson after the election said: 'They want to squeeze everyone out of council housing – it's good for us, but not for the children: where are they going to live?' And: 'We started off with the council – what are my kids going to do?' These views couldn't confound more emphatically the Conservative claims to have effected a revolution in people's ambitions. These people can't envisage that their children will ever be able to buy a house on the free market. They have no expectation of upward mobility for the next generation – the advancement, the self-improvement that Mrs Thatcher wants people to want.

5

Health Care

The main attraction of private health care is being able to jump the queues and not have to hang around. Time is so important nowadays. To take the morning off work to go to hospital doesn't look very good at work.

In health as with other services, the question of whether to 'go private' is usually seen as value-free, 'natural', a matter of increased purchasing power. In our discussion groups, Jonathan, who voted Conservative in 1987, said: 'I think you would naturally do it, because the more money you've got the more you try to improve, or think you improve. You might not get a better operation, but you might get it quicker. You might get your own anaesthetist and your own surgeon.'

When I drafted my first outline for this book, a month after the 1987 General Election, I excluded one thing from the triumph of individualism that the third Thatcher victory was supposed to represent. The book would look at why individualist solutions were in the ascendant in every area of public policy – 'except the National Health Service'. At the 1982 Conservative Party conference which served as the opening 'photo opportunity' of the 1983 hustings, Margaret Thatcher had announced that 'the NHS is safe with us', and this warranty had been repeated to the point of tedium ever since. The government's critics may not have agreed that it was, but the government seemed determined to try to present itself as a defender and improver of the NHS. Despite energetic cries of 'wolf!' from the opposition, the individualist solution of encouraging private health insurance by allowing people to opt out of funding the NHS was simply not on the agenda.

After the 1987 election, however, things changed. There is a much greater urgency in the debate about the health service:

urgency on the government's side as it seeks politically acceptable ways out of the collectivist impasse in which it clearly sees itself trapped, and urgency among its critics, who are crying 'wolf!' more sincerely than ever. The ideologues of the New Right have laid siege to the idea that the British people are unshakeably committed to their NHS, 'the envy of the world'. Whereas before the siege resembled that of a church, it now looks less like sacrilege. The sacredness of the institution and its Nicene Creed ('We believe in a health service for all according to need, free at the point of demand') has been commercialised, and agnosticism has been gaining ground.

Starting with Mrs Thatcher's declaration during the 1987 election campaign that going private enabled her to 'see the doctor I want on the day that I want at the time that I want', the Conservatives became bolder about their desire to promote private health insurance and to tie it into the bundle of Tory individualist values. In early 1988, junior health minister Edwina Currie made two controversial suggestions: one that old people should mortgage their homes to pay for health insurance, and the other that people should forgo spending on holidays for the same purpose. In the second case she was only echoing what Mr E, a Conservative bank clerk in Putney who last voted Labour in the 1970s, told us: 'Anyone with any money would [have private health insurance if they could afford it]. It would be the same as having a car or holidays abroad; if you've got the money, you would have it.'

As the research for this book went on, it became obvious that attitudes to health care were not qualitatively different from those to home ownership, share ownership and education. People feel much more warmly about the NHS than about state schools or council housing. But private provision is not usually frowned on – not even when it's thought of as damaging the NHS – and it is only natural to have it as personal prosperity increases. On the other hand, it is very rare for people to believe that it would be better if health care generally were provided privately.

Only one of our interviewees set out a case for private medicine in terms of Conservative *morality*, rather than Conservative affluence. Ms M, a committed Tory in Wolverhampton, said:

> I think that people who can afford it should pay a little. I think that's good for their pride. I don't think it's bad that people

should pay for prescriptions. The most valuable thing is nurses' and doctors' time, and it shouldn't be wasted. I don't begrudge anybody who is paying for [private health care]. What I do think is wrong is nurses being allowed to transfer to the private sector without having to pay back the cost of the training. And I do think they are badly paid. Private health care should pay for their doctors' and nurses' education. People have individual rights and everyone has responsibilities, you can't have one without the other.

Attitudes towards private health care haven't changed during the Thatcher decade, but support for the NHS has increased, probably because it now appears to be under threat. Only a small and unchanging minority think that private health treatment should be abolished, according to British Social Attitudes surveys: 10 or 11 per cent in 1983 and 1986. But a clear majority think that private treatment should not be allowed in NHS hospitals (57 per cent). There is some confusion about whether it is already banned (it isn't), because the most popular option in a differently worded question is that 'present arrangements are about right'. In general, people feel that they should live and let live, as in housing and education, although there is an obvious worry that private medical practice on NHS premises is likely to divert resources and doctors' loyalties from the public service. This is reinforced by the majority view (57 per cent again) that NHS doctors (GPs) should not be allowed to take on private patients.

On the other hand, nearly half the population – about 46 per cent – want to see private treatment encouraged, although half of them want it encouraged only outside the NHS. This is because, *provided it is kept out of NHS hospitals*, more people think that a private health sector is a good thing for the NHS (37 per cent) than think it a bad thing (19 per cent), and even more people think it makes no difference to the NHS (40 per cent).[1] 'Private health care is good as it shortens the NHS queues,' said one of Gould Mattinson's interviewees.

Gould Mattinson's post-election research reported a widespread feeling among both Labour loyalists and defectors that private health insurance would be a good thing if they could afford it, that it doesn't damage the NHS – on the contrary, it frees resources for it – and that people ought to be allowed to have it if they can afford it.

Because people do not believe that private medicine necessarily damages the NHS, support for – or toleration of – the private sector does not contradict overwhelming support for the principle of a universal National Health Service. 'It helps reduce the workload for the NHS,' said Ms O, who had private health insurance, a Wolverhampton Liberal convert from Labour in 1987. And yet Ms O, a former nurse, believed passionately in the principle of a national health service: 'It's bloody ridiculous to charge for staying in hospital. I mean, if I'm going to have an accident, a road accident or something, I might end up paying for it. It's just Maggie's way of getting rid of the NHS. Like they said they wanted to do some time ago.'

The British Social Attitudes surveys regularly test support for the idea of a universal health service by asking people if they would prefer the NHS to be restricted to the poor, with the tax savings helping or enabling the rest to pay for themselves. These surveys have only been carried out since 1983, but they show a large and unchanging majority against a selective health service. Interviewees were told: 'It has been suggested that the National Health Service should be available only to those with lower incomes. This would mean that contributions and taxes could be lower and most people would then take out medical insurance or pay for health care.' On average, 28 per cent supported this idea between 1983 and 1986; and it was opposed by 66 per cent.[2] This selective option is similar to one used in a question asked in a longer series asked by the free-market Institute of Economic Affairs (see p. 83). Its selective option attracted the support of 18 per cent of the population in 1978, which was more or less unchanged at 19 per cent in 1987. Its lower score is accounted for by the fact that its survey offered people three choices instead of two, but the basic message is clear. A selective NHS for the poor is unchangingly unpopular.

About 13 per cent of the population have health insurance, half of them through their work.[3] Most of these are social classes A and B, and mostly already Tory voters. But Gould Mattinson believe that a growing proportion of C1s and C2s now consider taking out private insurance as an option, regardless of their political views. When Gallup asked those who didn't have private insurance 'Would you consider joining a private scheme?' 32 per cent said yes and 68 per cent said no. The majority of those who say no do so because of the expense, according to Gould Mattinson's interviews. 'It's very nice if you've got the money, but frankly I haven't.' Only a few Labour voters claimed that even if they could afford it they wouldn't take out health insurance for ideological reasons. In our interviews, Mr U, a retired Labour voter in Glasgow, wouldn't take out private health insurance 'on principle'. He thought it fairly irrelevant: 'I don't think private health care is essential. But I wouldn't say it damages the NHS.' Gallup found that many more people would consider private insurance if it were provided by their employer (49 per cent would, 13 per cent said they still wouldn't, and 38 per cent didn't have an employer, and 44 per cent still would if it were 'offered by your employer on advantageous grounds').

Gould Mattinson found a rich seam of enthusiasm for private health insurance among at least a minority of ex-Labour voters. But it was a non-ideological enthusiasm: 'It's another expense but it's worth it not to have the worry.' 'I like a bit of luxury.' 'It gives you a quicker service.'

Most people had little idea of the cost, although it seems more accessible than private education. Mr N, a Wolverhampton engineering supervisor and a floating voter who voted SDP in 1987, said he would have private health insurance if he could afford it – 'everybody would'. But he didn't know how much it would cost: 'Offhand, no. BUPA's rather expensive, about £20 a month I think.' (In fact, the cheapest BUPA family policy would cost about twice that.) But he wasn't likely to take out private health insurance in the next ten years, 'unless the firm pays for it.'

People who thought that private health care complemented the NHS were, not surprisingly, more likely to have private health insurance or to say that they would if they could afford it. 'I don't think it takes anything away. I'm quite happy with the two-tier system as long as the NHS is there.'

Mr D was a good example of how support for private medicine could co-exist with support for the NHS:

> I would have thought, once it's all sorted out, that private health care will help out the NHS. Private health care costs a lot of money, [and] if the money is there, hopefully more people will be attracted to medicine which will mean, initially, more staff for the NHS.

I don't see anything wrong with private health at all. It could be that everybody may go private in the future and if that means little babies can get heart operations then it would be a good thing. But I still think that if you can't afford to contribute to health insurance then you should get free health care.

But he also supported the idea of private health care for other reasons:

No matter how much you improve the NHS people will still want private health care. When you have private health care it is totally different from the NHS. You make an appointment to see a doctor or a surgeon and he's there on time. You're paying for his time so he will tell you everything you want to know about your treatment and he will give you all his attention. You come out and you feel as if you've got something done. You can't get this on the NHS because they're overworked, that's the difference. If you go to hospital you could be there all day – I don't have time to do that. It's totally different going private, you get treated like a human being. It has nothing to do with the actual treatment, it's the convenience and the way you are treated. The patient–doctor relationship is totally different.

The family before politics

However, those who objected to private medicine would *also* have private health insurance if they could afford it, in most cases. 'Private health care definitely damages the NHS,' said a Putney clerical worker, Mr A, who thought of himself as Labour but who voted Alliance in 1987. 'Doctors and nurses get paid more in the private sector, so if they are good enough they move across, and the NHS is left short. I don't really agree with private medicine. I don't feel that people with more money than working class or poor people should be able to buy their way to the top of the waiting lists or get private treatment.'

But would he have private health insurance if he could afford it?

I could afford private health care now. There is a company scheme whereby you just pay in a certain amount each week, and many of my workmates do pay into BUPA. I think I would consider paying into the scheme in ten years' time, when I'm about forty. As you get older I think you have to take a more personal look at health care. Even though I believe in the health service, you've got to look after yourself as you start to get older. If something did happen and I had a bad illness, rather than wait a long time you could get treatment more quickly. I don't agree with private medicine, but as I get older I probably will subscribe to one of the schemes.

Mr H, a young lorry driver in Basildon and a Conservative convert from Labour in 1983, said: 'As far as I can gather, it takes away resources. You seem to hear about private patients using National Health Service equipment, but the service should really be only for NHS patients. I would have private insurance if it was a perk that went with my job. I've nothing against it, but I refuse to pay for it when we have a system like the National Health. [But] if the NHS got any worse we might have to consider private insurance.'

Mr K, a Labour-inclined non-voter, said:

I think the encouragement of private health care damages the NHS. The government is encouraging us to use private health schemes and they are bent on taking away resources from our National Health Service; it's bound to eventually go down hill. I'm not happy with the NHS as it is now. It is realistic to improve the NHS but it isn't possible under this present government and their way of doing things. The NHS needs a realistic amount of money, but it will only get it if we as a nation feel that the NHS is a priority. The money they've just earmarked for the NHS is just a rag on the wound. Our government is pushing us towards the American system, but whether or not they achieve it remains to be seen. It's a terrible system and I wouldn't want to see it here.

Asked if he would have private health insurance if he could afford it, he said:

If it comes to it, yes. We've all got to survive and we have to put that before our beliefs. But I wouldn't choose to if I don't have to. Paying for health care would mean you would get the best possible care. Not having to wait would be part of that. It's not possible to get the best possible care within our health service as it stands at the moment. One problem is the waiting lists. But there's also the problem of the abuse of staff and the overwork of staff, they can't possibly give you their best.

The same applied to having a private family doctor. 'If I could afford it, with any beliefs that I had, I would have the best for my family. My family would override any political ideas that I might have.'

Many of those who see the private sector as a drain on the NHS see this not as a reason for hostility towards the private sector but as an argument for more resources for the NHS. Mr E, a longstanding Conservative, said private health care

doesn't take resources away. It highlights that the health service is inadequate. Nurses wouldn't go from the NHS to the private sector if conditions in the national sector were as good as in the private. Nurses have just been sitting ducks for every government. When the bomb blew up in Brighton Mrs Thatcher and her Cabinet were very glad that a hospital was open just around the corner. I hope nothing like that happens again because that same hospital may well be closed.

Queue jumping

In one of those quirks of unrepresentative samples, the one really principled objection to private medicine came from Mr G, a machine operator in Basildon and a Conservative who had only voted Labour in local elections. 'I think it damages the health service. People who don't deserve to jump the queue get the treatment just because they can afford it. It's unfair that people can buy good health care. People don't want to get sick.' Would he have private health insurance if he could afford it? 'On principle, no I wouldn't. I don't believe in jumping the queue.'

A Gallup poll in March 1988 showed that there is substantial hostility to 'queue jumping'. Opinion divided equally, 48 per cent saying it was 'acceptable to jump the queue for treatment by going privately' and 45 per cent that it was unacceptable (7 per cent didn't know). This is the awkward question that divides individualists from collectivists more sharply than any other, but Mr G was the only one to mention it spontaneously.

Mr B, a Labour-inclined skilled manual worker, also objected strongly to private medicine, but on more practical grounds. He agreed that private health care damaged the NHS.

> Yes, definitely. It has been publicised that NHS equipment has been used by the private sector and that means it is not available for NHS use. And it takes doctors and nurses away from the health service. I totally disagree with private medicine and wouldn't have anything to do with it. Out of my wages each week I pay into the NHS. I don't see why I should have to pay into a private scheme just because the government has cut back on the National Health Service. It is realistic to improve the health service and the government should do so.

His more utilitarian attitude was underlined when he was asked if he believed in the guiding philosophy behind the NHS, of free health care for all according to need. 'Up to a point,' he said. 'I disagree with foreigners coming into this country and taking the NHS for a free ride.'

Ms Z, a Scottish army wife who voted SDP in 1987, used a similar argument for not having private health insurance: 'Because we pay for it through National Insurance and I don't see why I should pay for it again.' She thought it possible to improve the NHS so that no one would want private health care: 'Yes. Or so that no one *should* need it.'

Some people thought the private health sector was too small to affect the NHS. Ms E, a retired nurse, said: 'I don't think [private health care] damages the NHS. There is such a low percentage of people who can afford it, it really is only for the high fliers.' She identified the government as the main cause of damage. 'The health service is being undermined by the government. It's pushing more for private health care. And now they're going to make people pay for dental and eye checks. Instead of pushing preventative medicine, they will make us worse off. We'll all soon be forced to take out private health insurance.'

But she wouldn't choose to have private health insurance even if she could afford it.

When you go into a National Health hospital everything is checked and double checked. If you go into a private hospital things are completely different. They try to make as much money as possible and there isn't the same kind of care as in a National Health Service hospital. In NHS hospitals you are dealing with people of high integrity. People wouldn't choose to go private if they knew what went on behind the scenes.

She agreed that it was realistic to improve the NHS so that no one would want to go private. 'If the waiting lists were cut down I don't see why anyone would want to go private.'

The waiting list is the principal spur to 'going private'. Mr A: 'If I knew I wouldn't have to wait for treatment I wouldn't bother to pay into BUPA.' A Gallup poll in March 1988 reported that 'less waiting time' was cited by half of those with private health insurance as a reason for joining a scheme; only a quarter mentioned 'higher quality treatment' and just one in ten mentioned 'smarter surroundings'.

This is exploited by the private health insurance companies, especially PPP (Private Patients Plan) for its low-budget 'Private Hospital Plan', which provides private treatment only if you have to wait longer than six weeks on the NHS. The advertising for this insurance scheme realises that the fear of waiting lists is a strong selling point, but doesn't want to put people off by portraying the NHS as ghastly. 'For emergency treatment, few health systems can equal our NHS,' it says. 'This plan combines the best of the NHS with the advantages of private hospital care.' Another leaflet makes use of the common belief that private health care helps to take the burden off the NHS. 'This private medical plan eases the strain on the Health Service by working alongside it.'

As in other things, Ms D is blunt about the advantages of ruthless individualism. 'The main attraction of private health care is being able to jump the queues and not have to hang around. Time is so important nowadays. To take the morning off work to go to hospital doesn't look very good at work.' But, on the other hand, 'I wouldn't use private medicine if I didn't have to wait hours for my appointment. I do believe in free health care for all. But some people will always want private medicine. You feel that because you're paying you're going to get something better.'

Di, in our group discussions, was a shade more apologetic in putting Mrs Thatcher's doctor, day and time requirement: 'If I needed something urgently for myself or my family, probably, yes. Only for the quickness of getting the attention that I needed, because I didn't want to wait three years for a hip operation or something like that.'

Mrs Thatcher's election press conference confession was seized on by the Labour Party as a 'gaffe' (now a staple event in British election campaigns). Indeed, it was still being used by Labour in a party political broadcast in March 1988, but our evidence suggests that it could do her no harm. 'If she can afford it, good luck to her,' would be the typical response. Indeed, it may have helped her reputation as someone who goes after what she wants and gets it, her image of 'a get-up-and-go instead of a sit-back-and-wait-for-it Britain' (*The Times*, 9 February 1984).

'The envy of the world'

The importance of queue jumping, whether it is approved of or not, lies in the history of the NHS and its creation in the wartime climate of rationed austerity. The euphoria accompanying the setting up of the National Health Service in 1948 has intensified in the looking back, but it was still one of the most popular acts of the post-war Labour government. It was popular long before it happened. In 1939, 72 per cent of the public agreed that 'hospitals should be a public service supported by public funds', and only 22 per cent wanted to keep the pre-war system of private and charity medicine (Gallup).

This consensus deepened and broadened into the public ethic of shared austerity which dominated the war years and, with declining force, the decades afterwards. Between 1940 and 1945, most British people believed they shared a common (and good) purpose. It is partly the memory of the wartime social climate in which it was set up that conditions attitudes to the NHS today. One striking finding in our interviews was the length of people's political memories: many of their present-day political views were explained or defended by referring to events like the war, the creation of the NHS or Harold Wilson's first government.

We found an extensive feeling among those old enough to remember, and even among those that weren't, that the NHS was superlative when it was first set up. Ms M, a longstanding Tory in Wolverhampton: 'The NHS is what generations have dreamed of and worked for, and of the last two generations many haven't lived to see it in two world wars. The health service to my father was like the millennium.' The mythical status of the NHS as founded is contrasted with present shortcomings which make private health insurance understandable, inevitable and natural.

Mr C, a Putney pensioner who voted Alliance in 1987: 'The NHS was a great thing when it was created and I didn't think it would ever come to an end. But now she [Mrs Thatcher] is fighting like mad to kill it off. It was a wonderful service but now all our nurses are going and look who has done it. She underpays them, they're working all the hours that God gives us but they can't keep up.'

His wife, who voted Labour, shared the same sense of historical doom: 'They're closing all these hospitals, how do they expect people to get better then? Babies are waiting for operations . . . we never heard of it in our time. We had nothing, not two halfpennies to rub together, we had bread and jam for our dinner when I was a child but the National Health Service was there. Nobody could be ill unless they went into hospital. We had very little then compared to what we have now but you could say there's no NHS left.'

Mr E, aged 60 and a Tory voter, said he agreed with the principle of a free health care system, but felt ambivalent.

There have been abuses in the past. I clearly remember when the health service was first introduced a neighbour who dived off down the road for a set of teeth, a deaf aid, a pair of spectacles and a wig. It was ridiculous, the wig was never worn, the deaf aid was never used and the spectacles were relegated to a cupboard. People wanted medicines for no reasons at all in many cases. People will always abuse something that's free.

All the same, the NHS had been reliable, and now was not. Asked if his attitude to the private health insurance would change if the NHS were improved, Mr E said: 'I don't know. There's always the feeling that [private health insurance] would be a safeguard, an insurance just in case you need it. You could once rely on the NHS, but not any more.'

In Glasgow Mr U, a retired Labour voter, thought the NHS could be improved: 'As it was instituted initially, it wouldn't be necessary for people to have private medicine.' Ms W, a retired ex-Labour voter, thought the NHS was 'in a terrible mess', although 'it was good when it started'.

Mr Y, another Scottish Labour voter, also retired, said:

> What the government wants is for us to go back to the way it was before the war – we couldn't do that. There were people who couldn't call the doctor out; they couldn't afford to call the doctor, so they just died at home. And it wasn't much then: half-a-crown or something to call a doctor out, but if you didn't have it, that was that. No, that was terrible.

Even Mr A in Putney, aged about 30, said: 'It should just be as it was years ago when there were very few private clinics and everything was done on the NHS, the way it should be. But it will never go back like that.'

The origins of the NHS also lay in an awareness of class division. Hence Mr C, the Putney pensioner: 'There always will be private health care no matter how much money you spend on the NHS. The people who want it are toffee-nosed. A lot of people want to be different from anyone else: "Oh we're private." You've heard it so many times. I don't think there's anything better than the NHS. I had an operation a few years back and all the care and attention I had was wonderful.'

Given the origins of the NHS in circumstances when the prevailing social values were those of shared austerity, it should not be surprising that the principle of a universal health service should come under stress, and have to be defended on new grounds, when austerity is no longer even a memory for many people.

Universality and contracting out

When the Roehampton discussion groups talked about 'going private', they agreed that it was desirable. 'It would be quicker, but more expensive,' said Ann. This prompted Lynn to suggest that

81

if private health insurance were taken out, 'people in work could save that money, couldn't they? We all pay National Insurance and could save that money. The thing is, you still have to pay your National Health – you have to pay both'. If you don't want National Health, then you should choose, and not pay that, and then pay for the BUPA or whatever.'

The rest of the group were then asked if they would like to contract out. They did not. Carol: 'My husband's in BUPA at work. But no, it's because he's in work. If he was unemployed, then what would you do? Then we wouldn't be able to afford to go privately, would we?' Janet: 'Sometimes I think it's a good idea. But then there was something on television a couple of weeks ago about America.'

The men had a similar discussion. David, a Tory hardliner, said: 'I think everybody should have choice to opt out.' Three people chorused at once: 'They've got a choice now.' 'No I mean completely opt out,' said David. Brian enquired sarcastically: 'You want to opt out without paying anything to National Health? Is there anything else you'd like to opt out of paying taxes on?' David responded: 'Why should I pay twice over?' Hugh replied: 'If you want to opt out of the National Health, after sixty-five they don't want to know you, these private health plans. Even if you had a good job, if you have one operation, you'd be skint afterwards if you had to pay for it. The National Health relies on a lot of good healthy people to pay for the few that have the operations.'

The question is whether people who undertake not to use the NHS should get up to 11 per cent of their taxes refunded, which is the proportion that is spent on the health service. In both groups, the 'contracting out' principle was a minority one, and this was confirmed by a Gallup poll in March 1988. Gallup asked: 'Do you think that people with private health insurance should or should not have their taxes reduced because they are not using the National Health Service?' Only 26 per cent said they should (of whom up to half have private insurance and might be expected to give this answer); 66 per cent said they should not, and 8 per cent didn't know.

That people don't want a selective NHS, in which the better off are *compelled* to contract out, has been established on p. 72. But two of the leading lights of the New Right wrote a book called *Welfare Without the State*, in 1987, in an attempt to prove that British governments of both parties had conspired against the people since the war to deny them 'choice' in the welfare state. The book analysed a series of opinion polls commissioned by the free-market think-tank the Institute of Economic Affairs, which were designed to demonstrate that most people would prefer to have their taxes refunded and buy their own health care and education. The Labour Party should be very grateful to the rather sinister-looking Lord Harris and his longstanding partner in lost causes Arthur Seldon for this great research effort. It must have been intensely frustrating for them to discover in their latest survey that, since the Conservatives came to power in 1979, fewer people have opted for the Institute of Economic Affairs answer.

In the case of both health and education, the survey asked its 2,000 interviewees to choose one of three options:

1. The state should take more in taxes, rates and contributions to pay for better or increased services which everyone would have.

2. The state should take less in taxes, rates and contributions to provide services only for people in need and leave others to pay or insure privately.

3. The state should continue the present service but allow people to contract out, pay less contributions and so on and use the money to pay for their own services.

Even in this biased survey, the proportion preferring the policy of allowing 'contracting out' of National Health Service (option 3) dropped from 54 to 44 per cent between 1978 and 1987. The proportion wanting 'contracting out' of education spending fell from 60 per cent in 1978 to 48 per cent in 1987. (The bias in the survey lies mainly in that these questions were asked just after one which effectively asked: 'How would you like the government to give you a lot of money?' And the form of option 3 implies having your cake and eating it: 'continue the present service' – 'but allow people to contract out'.)

Harris and Seldon's attempt to explain the drop in support for individual contracting out during the years of the touted Thatcher Revolution reads like a parody. In recent years, they say, 'public discussion on welfare policies has centred on the issue of inadequate state funding and the extent, if any, of "cuts" in public spending. The dominant "solution" proffered by Labour and Liberal politicians – as well as by bishops and others – has lately crystallised in the proposal for higher taxes to finance more generous provision of existing welfare services.'

They conclude: 'It would be surprising if this overwhelming weight of advocacy did not influence many people to express support for higher taxes to pay for better services' (pp. 22–3). That Harris and Seldon should think this the 'dominant' solution is not as surprising as it seems; they see themselves as lone campaigners against a post-war socialist conspiracy which has bound Labour and Tory governments alike, and they accuse Mrs Thatcher of not moving fast enough (p. 77). But that the British people can so easily be swayed by this 'heavy advocacy' from their true and underlying attachment to the principles of the free market is more surprising.

Swayed, however, they were. Support for the 'improved universal' option 1 rose by 10 points in the cases of both health and education during the Thatcher years, to 30 per cent and 25 per cent respectively in 1987.[4]

Summary

As with other forms of private provision, there is a common assumption among politically committed people of whatever persuasion that private health care goes with Conservatism. Ms V, a Labour-supporting widow in Glasgow, said: 'It's terrible what the government is doing to the NHS. My husband died of a heart attack and complications, but the way the nurses looked after him was wonderful, and the doctors, they did everything they could. My sister has BUPA, what for I don't know: she's never been ill in her life, and I explain how good the NHS was with [my husband] but it makes no difference. I think it's because she's a Tory.'

Enough evidence has now been amassed here to demolish the fallacy of that simple equation. Ms J, a Basildon Alliance voter, provides a good example of how attitudes really work. She agreed that private health care damaged the NHS: 'If you've got a National Health appointment you seem to have to wait months and months. But if you go private you get in to see the same specialist in a couple of weeks. If he could see you then as a private patient, why couldn't he see you when you've been waiting on the National Health?' She nevertheless had private health insurance.

Although we are covered by private insurance we've never used it. Although when my husband had a bad ankle we almost went private. We waited eighteen months to see a specialist at Basildon Hospital – eighteen months! We went back to see our doctor while we were waiting and we told him we were in BUPA. We were in the process of going through BUPA when my husband's name came up. In the end we didn't have to use it, but we were going to because we were waiting for so long.

And she still supported the NHS. 'I don't think you should have to pay to get something as basic as health care. I think they've got to do something about the NHS because if they don't, in a few years time, it will be non-existent. I think the cuts are making the service worse, not more efficient. You've got all these nurses leaving and the only thing that's going to make them stay is more money.'

As with education, the decision to go private is normally regarded as something people do when they are well off enough, and is rarely seen as a political act. The difference between health and education is in the quality of the state health service. The NHS is – much more clearly than in education – the most efficient way of providing the service. Levels of satisfaction with the NHS are extraordinarily high, with big majorities 'very satisfied' with all aspects of the care they had received except the food. Ninety-five per cent were satisfied or very satisfied with the nursing staff; 94 per cent with the medical treatment; 92 per cent with the accommodation; and 89 per cent with the standard of cleanliness. Even though only 63 per cent were satisfied with the food (and it frequently lags behind Tesco's in its awareness of what foods are healthy and unhealthy), a larger majority, 69 per cent, were opposed to 'hotel' charges for food and beds (Gallup, March 1988). Support for the idea of hotel charges has increased in the past thirty years – in 1960, 80 per cent disagreed with charging patients for food – but not enough to undermine the consensus that the NHS should provide total care. Health insurance is often seen as a 'luxury' on top of excellent NHS provision, or in the event of unlikely contingencies.

Opposition to charges is balanced by a willingness to pay extra for collective benefit: the same Gallup poll reported that 59 per cent were prepared to pay more in taxes, if it were 'earmarked to increase spending on the NHS', and half of them were willing to pay more than £1 a week. Waiting lists reinforce support for collective provision just as much as they enhance the desirability of opting out.

6

Trade Unions

I would join a union if it was for self-gain, but I don't think I would gain anything. If I needed help I'd go to a Citizens' Advice Bureau.

The Conservative government claims that its reforms of trade union laws have not only been an unqualified success in improving industrial relations but have also 'transformed' the economy and by implication people's attitudes. 'Tory reforms have transformed a lame duck economy into a bulldog economy,' said Margaret Thatcher in the 1987 election campaign (2 June 1987). 'Prosperity in industry depends upon peace in industry – and what a transformation there has been in industrial relations' (9 June 1987).

There have been two main measures: the ban on secondary action (that is, picketing or striking at a company not directly involved in a dispute), and the requirement for secret pre-strike ballots. Other measures, such as those forcing union leaders to be periodically and directly elected, and ballots on closed shops, have had less impact, or, in the case of ballots on financial support for the Labour Party, have been a failure.

The image of trade unions was at its worst during the last Labour government, according to regular Gallup and MORI surveys. But even at their worst, just after the Winter of Discontent of public sector strikes in 1978/9, most people thought, 'generally speaking, and thinking of Britain as a whole, that trade unions are a good thing'. In July 1979, 51 per cent said they were a good thing, 36 per cent a bad thing, and 13 per cent didn't know. Since then trade unions have been regarded much more favourably; in 1987, 71 per cent said unions were a good thing, a 33-year high. Whether or not they are a good thing is clearly related to whether people think 'trade unions have too much power in Britain today'. MORI regularly asks people whether they agree or disagree with that statement, and there has been a huge change in people's replies under the Conservatives. In 1977 and 1979, people agreed that unions were too powerful by a majority of 41 per cent; in 1987, people *disagreed* by a majority of 20 per cent.

If attitudes towards trade unions have changed, there has certainly been no 'transformation' in the attitudes of trade union members themselves to the basic principle of trade unionism. There has been no significant change since the start of MORI's series in 1975 in the proportion of trade union members agreeing that 'trade unions are essential to protect workers' interests'. In 1979, 88 per cent agreed and 10 per cent disagreed; in 1987, 88 per cent agreed and only 5 per cent disagreed.

Gould Mattinson's post-election research found that, in the abstract, unions are regarded by some ex-Labour voters and many 'soft' Labour voters as a negative force, politically and economically. They feel that, given the chance, unions would wield power against the interests of the country. 'There'd be massive increases in wage claims and inflation would go straight up again.' 'All the good would go out of the window in six months.' 'They'd hold the country to ransom again.' 'Don't believe in them – stranglehold on the country.' (All C1 Labour-to-Conservative defectors.)

This was backed up by our own interviews.

Unions were too powerful before. In the days of the Labour government – this is one of the reasons why I stopped voting Labour – if they wanted to do something they had to invite all the union leaders to have a union meeting, then they'd have a Cabinet meeting, then another union meeting. And if they said no, that was it. It got to the stage where they were running the country. They brought the government down, they brought Heath down. You can't have that, it isn't democracy. The unions became the government under Labour, they were a secondary government. We haven't got that now. (Mr D, Putney union member, Conservative in 1987.)

Gould Mattinson reports that ex-Labour voters are, as a result, keen on the Conservatives' earlier trade union laws. 'Maggie won't stand the unions – she's put them in their proper place.' The banning of secondary picketing is particularly popular. 'People should stick to fighting their own battles.' But they also report a feeling among all but firm Tories that further anti-union laws would be unnecessary or wrong. 'It's gone far enough now – the balance is about right.'

Neither Gould Mattinson's nor our own interviewees felt that unemployment had played a part in tilting the balance of power in industry against the unions. In part this represents a triumph of demonisation rather than of individualism – in linking the idea of union leaders being 'out of touch with the workers they represent' (with which even a majority of union members agree) to ballots, and linking ballots to making 'the unions' less powerful.[1]

There was widespread support for secret, pre-strike ballots among our interviewees, with the name of Arthur Scargill, president of the National Union of Mineworkers, coming up again and again as the personification of everything that is undemocratic about trade unions. 'I do agree with the legislation on strike ballots. I do not believe that someone like Scargill should bring a union out without a ballot. I think the unions are democratic enough now, although the left wing can still get out of hand sometimes. The only good thing that has come out of this government for the unions is the secret ballot. It has given the unions back to their members. People like Scargill have tried to monopolise power in the past' (Mr A, Labour identifier, voted Alliance 1987). The use of a Conservative slogan ('giving the unions back to their members') by this man, quite hostile to the Tories, illustrates the effectiveness of the government's propaganda, but also how it reflected the way people already saw trade unions.

'Secret ballots are a good thing. In the past voting was influenced because there was no secrecy' (Mr B, non-voter in 1987, non-union member). 'Unions are all about the members, not half-a-dozen people who say they represent the membership. Before the ballots, strikes were called by the very militant [people] who bothered to turn up to the meetings. The rank and file didn't run the unions, they were run by people like Mr Scargill' (Mr D, union member and Conservative voter). 'Secret ballots are a good idea. A postal ballot would be an even better idea, then you could be sure that it will be fair' (Mr C, retired former union member, Alliance voter).

A brief digression into history, however, shows up the flaws in the claim that it was undemocratic trade unions' bullying of their members in the 1970s that produced a surge of support for laws on ballots in the 1980s. Despite the public image of trade unions being at a low ebb during the 1970s, there was actually an increase in the proportion of people who felt they had 'a say' in their trade union between 1973 and 1978.[2] How can this opinion poll finding be reconciled with the widespread belief that union leaders are out of touch? One possibility is that it reflects a greater self-confidence among union members, which raised expectations which the Tories proved better at satisfying and claiming credit for than the unions themselves.

Certainly unions did not lead the way in adapting their structures and procedures to a more assertive notion of democratic rights. There was during the 1960s and 1970s an increase in people's self-confidence in their individual rights as citizens which might be regarded as a pre- and non-Thatcherite individualism. This was reflected by the ex-Labour voters we interviewed as a hostility to voting by a show of hands. Mr G, a Conservative voter who was once a Transport and General Workers Union shop steward, said:

> If you go to a union meeting and there are a hundred people there, men like Scargill can more or less force men to vote a certain way if it's by a show of hands. They may not want to vote that way, but they know there will be trouble afterwards if they don't. It was blackmail. When I was a shop steward for the T and G, I persuaded men to do things they didn't want to do. You could send someone to Coventry, and that was a bad thing, if they didn't toe the line.

Ms J, a Basildon Alliance voter and ex-union member, expressed the same anxiety: 'The ballot is a good idea, definitely better than a show of hands. A lot of people will not want to vote against something their mates are supporting. And there's no doubt that some people were intimidated if they voted the "wrong" way.' Mr H, a union member who switched to the Conservatives in 1983, said: 'I don't think they should all stand there and have to put their hands up. If there are one or two who vote a different way they can be picked on later.'

But opposition to unfair pressure being put on union members does not imply lack of popular support for strong and effective action when workers have a 'just' cause. There is no indication that the Conservatives' attempts to enforce the 'right to work' of minorities in a workforce have much support, except in cases like the 1984–5 miners' strike when because there was no national ballot there was sufficient doubt as to whether those who wanted to strike were actually in a majority.

Asked if he had ever been on strike, for example, Mr P, an aggressive Thatcherite in Wolverhampton, said: 'I have, but not with this company. I have before. And no, I didn't agree with it, but that's democracy.' Mr A, a clerical worker who thought of himself as Labour although he voted Alliance in 1987, said: 'The last time I was on strike was about three years ago. I agreed with the decision because the company had broken a wage agreement. We were given virtually no choice. We came out for a weekend and more things happened over that weekend than had happened in eighteen months of negotiation.'

Even Mr B, a non-voter who was 'not in a trade union because I disagree with trade union policies' and whose non-union company 'runs with no trouble at all', said: 'It depends on the situation you find yourself in. If the governors of the company are taking you for a right old ride and that is the only way then, yes, strike action is justified. But I've never found myself in that position and I could never see it happening.'

A Conservative lorry driver, Mr H, said: 'I'm in a trade union because it is a closed shop at work. I wouldn't have joined if I'd had a choice. I was told that if I wanted the job I would have to sign a union membership form first. At first I did resent it, I don't think you should be compelled to join any union. But then I had some trouble and I've been able to put my hand up and shout "help", and they've come along and kicked management back into place. I've been converted to trade unionism.'

Although a Conservative voter, he saw work as a conflict between class interests, and his opposition to strike action was purely pragmatic. 'I've never been on strike. I am against strike action because it's silly. You never make the money you lose up again. The miners is a classic. They lost homes, cars, everything, for a principle. I think it's better to work to rule. At least you're still getting paid. I think getting together and making a point is more effective. It's better to send the steward upstairs to request bits and pieces.'

Ms J, the Alliance woman, had similarly been converted. 'I used to be in a trade union when I worked in the office. The girls in the office fought to be able to join the union. The girl I worked with was the area shop steward. She said: "Come and join, it'll help us to gain acceptance from management." I joined and it was good, they did get us our pay rises. Without the union we would have just had to go along with management.' So she too saw the workplace in terms of conflict, a conflict in which solidarity was an effective weapon.

She also had pragmatic objections to striking, rather than objecting to strikes *per se*.

> I think Maggie Thatcher has taken too much power away. They [the unions] are frightened now to do anything because she threatens to put them inside and all the rest of it. I think the miners' strike was very sad. They achieved very little after all that time out. Their families were on the breadline. Striking is rarely worthwhile. Negotiating and working to rule are much more effective. Striking just makes the other side even more determined not to give in.

What is often overlooked about people's attitudes towards trade unions is their self-interested nature. For politically aware observers, trade unions may represent the practical application of collective principle, and the solidarity of unionised workers can be interpreted as idealistic and ideological when in fact, for the people we interviewed, trade unions were useful for what you could get out of them. Ms D, a Putney personal assistant who abandoned Labour for the Tories in 1983, put it most bluntly: 'I would join a union if it was for self-gain, but I don't think I would gain anything. If I needed help I'd go to a Citizens' Advice Bureau.' It is worth noting *en passant* that Citizens' Advice Bureaux are examples of another form of collective self-help: she wouldn't go to a solicitor. Having criticised the trade unions for the three-day week (in 1973), which she described as 'the unacceptable face of trade unionism', she went on to add: 'I could see myself going on strike if it was a small company and you could hold them to ransom, then I would go for it.'

Others who were union members were a little less direct. 'With a union, if you want anything, you've got them to back you up,' said Mr L, a Wolverhampton factory storeman in the AEU, the engineering union, and a first-time Tory voter in 1987. 'They're useful, but sometimes you're in this union, you pay all your contributions and that and they don't do anything for you.' So although he recognised the need for solidarity – 'You've got to stick together, get together, when you're working in a factory' – it was highly conditional.

For several interviewees, even this self-interested solidarity was minimal. For Mr N, a Wolverhampton SDP foreman, the advantages of union membership – in his case, the tiny Black Country based National Union of Lock and Metal Workers – were reduced to the 'administrative' and the safety net. 'You need a spokesperson, for the sake of good management as much as anything else. And you've got professional help if you need it.' Even Mr P, the aggressive Wolverhampton Thatcherite, accepted the argument for a safety net on grounds of self-interest. 'I'm a member [of the Transport and General Workers Union] because I want to be. If you're off sick you can get help. If you have an accident it would cost you a fortune to get a lawyer for yourself. It makes sense.' These 'self-interested collectivist' attitudes back up John MacInnes's argument that 'there is a sense in which the British working class has always been prone to "middle class" and individualist ways of thinking, and far from conflicting with the tradition of adversarial industrial relations – a tradition which is still very much intact – it is a basic part of that tradition' (*Thatcherism at Work*, p. xv).

Gould Mattinson found that many union members (among C1/C2 'soft' Labour and ex-Labour voters) had a very weak sense of belonging to their own union. This was even more marked among women, who are alienated by most aspects of active trade unionism. Most found it hard to articulate the benefits they derived from membership beyond the most basic concept of insurance. 'The only reason I stay in is in case I have an accident.' 'They're there in case anything goes wrong – otherwise you don't give it much thought.'

The weak sense of belonging seems to be linked to two criticisms – of unions' inability to get results on pay and conditions, and of union leaders. Hence the circular logic of people's support for Conservative anti-union laws and complaints about their own union's weak bargaining position. 'Management don't have to talk to the unions now. They don't even have to *know* them.' This reinforces the idea, although still a minority one, that unions are out of date. 'Unions were created in the last century – it doesn't belong in the 1980s – a residue of the class system.' But Gallup found that in 1985 only 22 per cent agreed that 'trade unions may have been needed at one time in Britain, but not any longer,' and 68 per cent disagreed. And our interviews showed (p. 91) that many people

93

still think of their workplace in terms of a class conflict between management and workers.

All the same, people often associate big workforces, trade unions and 'labour' as the underdog with a 'them and us' world which existed only in the past. Shiona Fox-Ness, a self-employed, self-confessed Labour 'traitor' on Channel 4's *Loves Labour Lost* programme (6 January 1988), said:

> Coming back to Leith, now, it just seems there's a lot less people here. I remember passing on the bus, going to school or something like that, and there would be hundreds of workers pouring out of the docks and they'd all rush and there'd be massive queues at the bus stop, and the same at printing works and the mills and things like that, you just don't see these masses of people any more. In fact I don't even know if the working class is there any more; it seems to be missing. I think it's disappearing, like [the connection between] the Labour Party and the working class.

Non-unionism flourishes in small companies where the solidarity of large numbers in one workplace seems like newsreel history. 'I think in many of the big companies strikes are called for no good reason,' said Putney non-voter Mr B, a skilled machinist in a small company making car parts.

> I work in a non-union company and it runs with no trouble at all. A union in there would make no difference at all. I just can't see the need for unions in this day and age. Unions get too involved with politics rather than with union work. Problems can be solved before the need to strike if management and workers are prepared to give and take a little bit. I've never been on strike. If we've got problems, we go to the foreman and, if he can't help us, we go and see the managing director. I think to start with there was a need for trade unions but in these days, in the bulk of places, companies are run in a fair way.

It may be true that the changing pattern of work, split up into smaller units, is changing the nature of trade unionism. But, as John MacInnes points out, the 'Japanisation' of British working practices and industrial relations shouldn't be exaggerated. The wave of unrest in the car industry in the spring of 1988, although it was rather unconvincingly dubbed the 'Spring of Discontent' by some press commentators, did indicate the limits of the Thatcher Revolution in industrial relations. It confirmed that the main cause of the alleged transformation of attitudes on the British shopfloor was the 1979–82 recession rather than the acceptance of the principle of management's 'right to manage'. Continuing high unemployment acts as a restraint on labour assertiveness, but the steady rise in productivity has increased workers' demands for a fair share in the resulting profits.

Shopfloor workers at Ford articulated these demands in a strike in February 1988, the first all-out stoppage at Ford for over five years. *The Guardian* (9 February) reported a driver, George Riley, as saying he and his colleagues were 'wanting some reward for the efforts we have made over the past two years in increasing production'. Richie Rowlands, chairperson of the joint shop stewards, said: 'We don't make rash decisions, and no one enjoys being in dispute. We only have this job to sustain our families and try to exist. Our record over the past five years speaks for itself, with production climbing. We are not asking for trouble, but want our aspirations met.'

The same point was less subtly put by Bill, an assembly worker quoted by *The Independent*: 'The government's asked people to be more efficient. Ford has done that – through us. We've put in the graft. We want paying accordingly. If that means a long dispute, so be it.' (It didn't: the dispute was settled when Ford agreed to their main demand a few days later.)

If unions are changing, the importance of the Ford strike was to show how much their members' attitudes remain the same. People see work in terms of a conflict between employer and employee over their respective shares of the profit from their labour. And, if they feel that they are entitled to a greater share than employers voluntarily concede, they see solidarity through trade unions as the way of having their 'aspirations met'.

Cynicism and sectionalism

The unpopularity of trade unions in the 1970s is a good example of how the idea that there is a simple division between 'individualism' on the one hand and 'collectivism' on the other breaks down. Trade unions often work on a third principle, that of 'sectionalism'. In their review of their findings on the subject of trade unions, Gallup's Gordon Heald and Robert Wybrow comment on the 'feeling of alienation and cynicism pervading the views of the British public' (*The Gallup Survey of Britain*, p. 146). Because people often see unions cynically in terms of what they personally can get out of them, they become vehicles for collective selfishness. The experience of the 1970s made it very clear that the interests of one section of the working class could conflict with the interests of another, especially if one was in the public sector and the other wasn't. Trade unions were seen as the expression of this sectionalism, and therefore they were thought to be against the true collectivism of the common interest of the country as a whole. Hence John MacInnes' conclusion that 'the problems of the 1970s perhaps stemmed from too little rather than too much collectivism in British industrial relations' (*Thatcherism at Work*, p. xiv).

It was, as the transport workers' leader Jack Jones said at the time, a tragedy that the unions didn't understand this themselves. In 1977 he pleaded unsuccessfully with his union's national conference not to throw out the Social Contract with the Labour government and return to 'free collective bargaining'.

If you in this conference defeat composite 1A you will make trouble ten times more for years to come. You give the prize for what has been done not to the working people of Britain but you hand it over to, yes, Thatcher, Joseph and Heseltine and all of that ilk of privilege. The benefits of North Sea oil are on the horizon. The benefits of a stronger balance of payments are also on the horizon. And they are going to the party of privilege. Instead of being free, you will put the mighty in the seat and kick the people of low degree in the teeth. That is the danger.[3]

Instead of trying to resolve sectional conflicts in the name of some notion (for example, Jack Jones's) of a common national interest, the Conservatives have washed their hands of them, claiming that the national interest will look after itself. The public sector workers with industrial muscle have been broken or warned off, particularly by the 1984–5 miners' strike. Some public sector workers have been transferred to the private sector. 'Many of the troubles governments faced in the 1970s stemmed from their attempts to maintain full employment as a priority,' comments John MacInnes. 'In abandoning this goal Thatcherism has had its greatest impact on the British industrial relations system; not by undermining trade union bargaining power but by taking the unemployed out of the reckoning and letting employers and workers maximise their own returns regardless of the consequences for the aggregate level of employment' (*Thatcherism at Work*, p. xiv).

This is only likely to increase cynicism, or 'informed fatalism' as Marshall, Newby, Rose and Vogler (or one of them at least) calls it in *Social Class in Modern Britain* (p. 143). Their survey suggests that 'the collectivism of our respondents . . . reflects the pursuit of self-interest rather than collective improvement'. They comment that, given that social inequality and class divisions are 'perceived to be unjust, but are accepted as largely unalterable facts of life', this is 'an entirely pragmatic response'. Most working-class people, therefore, are sceptical about solidarity with other members of their class, not because they don't want the condition of the working class generally to be improved, but because they don't think it works.

The Conservatives have encouraged this fatalism, by denying that people can be public spirited (without having 'money as well', as Mrs Thatcher said of the Good Samaritan). They have denied that society could successfully be organised on more cooperative, collectivist lines. Thus there is a wider than usual gap between government and people. The government thinks it is not possible because it is ideologically undesirable; the people think it is not possible despite being ideologically desirable. 'People are often aware of alternatives,' conclude Marshall *et al.*, 'but they are, on the whole, resigned to the fact that they can do little or nothing to help achieve these. Our findings suggest that contemporary British society lacks a moral order, and that its cohesion is rooted more in resignation and routine than consensus and approval' (p. 143).

Summary

Trade unions in Britain were considered 'too powerful' in the 1970s, although the cynicism of the electorate meant that when Prime Minister Edward Heath asked in 1974 'Who governs

Britain?' they replied 'The unions do' and elected a Labour government, partly in the belief that the Labour Party would get on better with the unions and hence run the economy better.

However, the electorate still accepted the case, put by the Conservatives, for pre-strike ballots, as a means of reducing the power of union leaders, if not unions themselves. Most of our ex-Labour-voting interviewees opposed strike action, but on the pragmatic grounds that it was usually ineffective; they were not anti-strike in principle.

Attitudes to trade unions are pervaded by a fairly cynical 'instrumentalism', in that people see unions in terms of what they personally can get out of them.

This cynicism is only increased by the gap between what the government wants people to think and what they actually think. Support for some of the Tory trade union reforms – those couched in the language of democracy – doesn't mean that people accept the whole package of individualism. The government, for example, believes that trade unions, even 'responsible' ones, impede economic progress by distorting the labour market and that individuals and minorities should be encouraged to break strikes. The people, on the other hand, are more likely to agree that 'employees need strong trade unions to protect their interests' than to disagree.[4] And, as long as there is a democratic majority for a strike, in a secret ballot, most people support the right of the majority at least to discourage a minority from strike breaking.

7

Share Ownership

I don't feel there is anything wrong, even though it might be
a Tory idea, in making a quick killing in something like BT.
People knew the price was going to go straight up.

The Conservatives stumbled on the policy of privatisation almost by
accident in 1982. Until then it meant local councils being forced to
put building work out to tender. Free-market flat-earthers had been
writing pamphlets since the 1950s arguing that the government
should sell all publicly owned assets to the private sector. But it
wasn't just because Mrs Thatcher had a vision of 'rolling back the
frontiers of the state' that their arguments were picked up by the
Conservative government.

The 1979 Conservative manifesto only promised to return to
the private sector the aerospace and shipbuilding industries, which
Labour had just nationalised, and the National Freight Corpora-
tion. None of these raised significant amounts of money. It was
when Britoil, the public-sector North Sea oil company, was sold
off for £500 million in 1982, as part of a job lot of anomalies
like Amersham International (part of the UK Atomic Energy
Authority), that it was suddenly realised that an unfashionable
piece of ideological dogma could be useful.

Chancellor Geoffrey Howe had a serious problem on his hands,
because at that stage the radical Tory hands-off, tax-cutting administration had done nothing but raise taxes. And at the time, the
£500 million raised by Britoil was the equivalent of a halfpenny
off income tax for a year. When Margaret Thatcher took office,
taxes took 38 per cent of Britain's national income. By 1982 that
figure had shot up to over 46 per cent. It was not brought down
below 45 per cent until Nigel Lawson's pre-election tax-cutting
Budget in March 1987.[1] The government's boasts about tax cuts

are believed partly because the tax burden has been shifted from income tax to VAT, and partly because since 1982 earnings for people in work have been steadily rising. But if it hadn't been for the huge amounts raised by selling British Telecom and British Gas in particular, £3,600 million and £5,200 million in 1984 and 1986, the record of this 'tax-cutting' government might have looked very different.

With the flotation of Jaguar in 1984, the Conservatives stumbled across another advantage of privatisation. There was a near riot in the City as professionals and for the first time large numbers of non-City slickers scrambled to apply for eight times as many shares as were on offer. A fixed-price share offer to the general public could generate instant profits for buyers, thus guaranteeing a successful sale and cementing support for the transfer of corporations from public to private sectors. As long as the offer is priced at a sufficiently low level, the procedure can almost guarantee instant profits for anyone who has or can borrow a few hundred pounds and is capable of filling in a form. This helped encourage very large numbers of small buyers to come forward to take up the British Telecom offer three months later. Because the government was worried that City markets wouldn't be able to find £3,600 million in one go, it wanted those small investors for financial as well as political purposes. A further incidental advantage for the Conservatives was the opportunity to produce a lot of expensive sub-party-political advertising for the virtues of private share ownership.

Until the flop of the British Petroleum offer in October 1987, the device seemed wonderfully successful, with Conservatives trumpeting the education of the British people in the virtues of 'popular capitalism', and their critics bemoaning the public greed of the queues jostling in narrow City streets for what were effectively handouts given to people by a kind of means test in reverse – the richer you are the more help you get.

But does it all make any difference to people's basic political values? The answer seems to be that it does not.

Early data from the 1987 British Election Study suggest that people who had bought privatisation share issues were no more likely to vote Conservative than those who had not. Of course, as with council house sales, Conservatives are more likely to buy privatisation shares in the first place, because they are more likely to be able to afford them – but buying shares did not make Labour or Alliance supporters switch to the Tories. This is supported by Harris Research's exit poll, which reported a 2-point fall in the Conservative vote among people who had acquired shares since 1983, as against a 1-point fall among those who had not (John Curtice, *New Society*, 19 June 1987).

A clue to the attitudes lying behind this statistic can be found in this comment from Mr A in Putney, who thought of himself as Labour despite voting Alliance in 1987:

> I took the shares out in my own company because we got a special deal. It was in my own interest. I don't really dabble on the stock market, although I was going to buy some BP shares, but like everybody else I got out in time. I was tempted by British Telecom, but I just didn't have the money at the time. I don't feel there is anything wrong, even though it might be a Tory idea, in making a quick killing in something like BT. People knew the price was going to go straight up. I wouldn't have held onto them if I had bought shares in BT, I would have sold them straight away to make a quick financial gain.

Gould Mattinson found – before the October 1987 stock market crash – that the majority of those who didn't own shares would consider buying them, regardless of voting intention. But they also found some ambivalence. Many Labour defectors, especially in clerical jobs (social class C1), were positive about privatisation because they liked the idea of workers owning shares in their own companies. 'When people own shares in the company they work for, they are more interested in their jobs and more concerned about the company.' 'It's a big incentive for the individual to work hard and that's good for business.' 'It creates a more responsible attitude. It has a big effect on strikes.' (All C1 Conservatives.) But when it comes to share ownership in general, 'surprisingly few endorsed the opportunity culture', although one C1 Conservative man said: 'Buying shares has given people a chance to bridge the gap [in society].'

Ex-Labour voters had mixed feelings about the big sell-offs. 'I'm not sure about British Gas – the things that we all use – surely the profits should go into reducing the cost to the consumer?' 'It's part of our heritage, isn't it?' 'If you've got a white elephant, fair enough, let someone else sort it out. But if you've got a profitable concern, why sell it off cheaply?'

As with trade unions, attitudes towards nationalisation have swung away from hostility in the course of the Thatcher governments. And, as with trade unions, this doesn't mean that underlying attitudes towards state ownership have changed. People could see no good reason at the end of the 1970s why certain things should be in the public sector, but by 1986 felt that privatisation had gone far enough.

In fact, the only time nationalisation was really popular in Britain was the early years of the post-war Labour government. Gallup asked in December 1945: 'Have you heard about the government's idea of nationalising coal, transport, electricity, and so on? Do you approve?'

	%
Yes	59
No	25
No opinion	11
Haven't heard	5

But by January 1948 further nationalisation was already unpopular. That of the iron and steel industries was opposed by 36 to 31 per cent (33 per cent didn't know), and became more unpopular, opposed by 51 to 28 per cent (21 per cent didn't know), by January 1949.

MORI has asked a consistent series of questions on nationalisation since 1973. The question asks whether 'All or some more industries should be nationalised; no more industries should be nationalised; or all or some of the nationalised industries should be denationalised.' Between 1973 and 1980, support for 'denationalisation' gradually increased, and since 1981 it has faded away again. In 1973, there was a small majority in favour of nationalisation (3 per cent); by 1980, there was a 21 per cent majority for denationalisation. By May 1987, support for and opposition to nationalisation was more or less evenly balanced, with 31 per cent wanting to retain the *status quo*.[2]

What's more, when MORI asked in December 1987 about specific industries that had not yet been sold off, high levels of hostility were revealed in every case.

'Do you support or oppose the government adopting the following policies? Selling [. . .] to private shareholders.'

	Water Authorities %	Elec. industry %	British Coal %	British Steel %	Post Office %
Support	22	34	33	35	27
Oppose	67	56	56	54	65

On the water and electricity industries, there were large majorities against privatisation at the time of the 1987 election, and an 8-point swing against the government's plans by the end of the year. Even the sale of British Coal and British Steel, which are not 'natural' monopolies, and which many might think more suitable for privatisation than telecommunications and gas, was substantially unpopular.

The argument that the profit motive is necessarily better than the public service motive has not been won: most views on the boundary between private and public sectors are pragmatic or indifferent. 'Nationalised industries used to be run just as well as the private sector. It's been done before. The basic essentials should be state-owned, things like heating, light and water. British Telecom should be privatised, but the others shouldn't be. I don't think [the government] needs to [control British Telecom's prices and profits]. The only problem there is that there's no competition' (Mr N, Wolverhampton foreman). 'I don't think it makes a lot of difference whether the state or the private sector owns a monopoly. British Telecom seems to have got worse since it was privatised, but it still seems to be making huge profits. Privatisation doesn't seem to have made a lot of difference to British Gas. Governments have forced up prices even though the gas or the electric have made huge profits. That shouldn't be allowed' (Mr D, self-employed Conservative, Putney).

Indeed, the arguments about monopoly and competition are the only technical aspects of the question that were discussed by our interviewees. And they were not approached in an ideological fashion. The fact of monopoly services was generally considered to be *both* an argument for public ownership *and* an argument for more competition. 'The monopolies should be run by the government for the benefit of everybody. Prices should be controlled because there is no competition. You are not in the position of being able to go elsewhere for the service' (Mr E, Conservative, last voted Labour in about 1974). 'The government should definitely control their prices and profits. I can't go anywhere else with my custom. I've

103

got to have my gas from Eastern Gas and my electric from Southern Electric' (Mr H, Conservative, last voted Labour 1979).

The essentially non-ideological nature of popular attitudes towards nationalisation – the relative indifference to the role of the state – was demonstrated by a controversy in 1986 over a Trades Union Congress survey which claimed that public ownership was overwhelmingly popular. The survey, carried out by National Opinion Polls, asked 'Which of this list of industries and services do you think should be publicly or privately owned?' and produced clear majorities for public ownership of everything on the list. This included a 71 to 21 per cent majority for public ownership of 'essential services like electricity, gas and water' (9 per cent didn't know). But another poll taken at exactly the same time by Survey Research Associates asked: 'As you may know, the government intends to privatise British Gas, that is, to sell shares in British Gas to the public. Do you support or oppose the decision to privatise British Gas?' This found 44 per cent supported privatisation and 29 per cent opposed it (27 per cent replied 'neither' or 'don't know').

So why did one poll find a 50-point majority for public ownership of the gas industry at the same time as the other found a 15-point majority for privatisation? As Peter Kellner pointed out in the *New Statesman* (12 December 1986), the two polls tell us much less about attitudes to state ownership than about responses to the word 'public'. The first poll contrasted 'public' ownership with 'private' ownership; the second contrasted 'the government' with 'the public' as owners of British Gas. People respond positively to the word 'public' – 'it implies democracy, the general good, us rather than them', says Kellner – and negatively to 'private'. The fact that the Survey Research Associates poll threw in the word 'privatise' on the 'public' side of the equation may help to account for the high 'neither'/ 'don't know' response. (Of course, National Opinion Polls' use of the phrase 'essential services' and its lumping together of all three services further biased its response in favour of public ownership, but the word 'public' is probably the most important factor.)

Hence the emphasis in the Conservative election campaign on 'selling shares to the public' and giving power to 'the people'. If MORI had asked about selling shares in the five industries on p. 103 to 'the public' instead of to 'private shareholders', support for privatisation would appear to be much higher. The power of language has been recognised for years by the providers of private health care and education, which often describe themselves as 'independent' hospitals and 'independent' schools (although with education meanings are further confused by the phrase 'public school').

The hard question is whether the Conservatives' bold use of the word 'privatisation' (originally an insult used against them) and their advocacy of private enterprise has changed the connotations of the word 'private' in people's minds. The use of 'the public' in the election campaign in 1987 suggests that the Conservatives didn't think they had won people over, that they weren't confident enough that they had broken down the associations of the word 'private' with privilege and class division. It is the 'public', after all, which denotes the collective interest of the people, while 'private' means precisely the individualism that is alleged to be dominant, and that is alleged to be the base of Conservative popularity.

As with other 'successful' Conservative policies, the acceptance by the electorate of specific policies on pragmatic or self-interested grounds does not always mean that the voters buy the 'free-market' ideology that politicians and political commentators assume are bundled in with them. But sometimes it does. One of our Putney interviewees seemed to have bought the whole package in this way, Ms D, a personal assistant who switched from Labour to Conservative in 1983. She used phrases from Conservative slogans of the 1987 election campaign to endorse the 'free market'. 'I think it's a good idea that a privilege like share ownership has now filtered down to ordinary people. Working-class people are now being given the chance to enjoy things that only the rich once had access to. It's the same with private education.'

Compare that with this bit of Mrs Thatcher's eve-of-poll speech, endlessly repeated throughout the 1987 election campaign. 'Home ownership, share ownership, choice in education – all these were once the privileges of the few. These are now being extended to the many.' This was also echoed by Ms J, a Basildon Alliance supporter:

> Something that was just once for the very rich has now filtered down; it's a good idea. I've got British Telecom and my husband has shares from his company's productivity deal; he gets so many each year. Plus he contributes to a share ownership scheme. I

do think shares are a good investment. I think it gives you an interest. I look at how my shares are doing every day in the paper. I like to see whether they've gone up or down. I didn't buy them for a quick profit, I intend to hold onto them. I think it does make them better companies if they are owned privately. State-owned companies are not given enough scope to improve themselves. I think they should now be left to get on with it themselves. The government shouldn't interfere.

Ms D similarly supported the rest of the free-market package:

I was in favour of privatisation, even though I couldn't afford to buy shares. The government shouldn't control prices and profits. They should be treated just like any other company. I'd need a lot of money before I'd invest in shares, unless it was the company I worked for. Then I would like a profit-sharing scheme. Workers should buy shares in their own company. Secretaries would use Tipp-Ex rather than throwing an envelope away – little things like that can save a lot of money at the end of a year. If I could buy shares in my company I would. I wouldn't work any harder, but my housekeeping would be better. Individuals would look after the purse strings and they wouldn't take the company for a ride.

The October 1987 crash suddenly reminded new shareholders of the risks of the stock market, and at least temporarily punctured the tentative confidence that Gould Mattinson had identified. 'You start to realise that all the big boys know what they're doing – and we've got no idea.' 'I want to sell my shares, but I don't know what to do.' 'We wish we'd kept our money where it was, really – in the savings bank.' 'It's hard to know what to do now, you hear so many different bits of advice.' And many of those non-shareholders who had said they would consider share ownership quickly dissociated themselves from the idea: 'Serves those yuppies right.'

Our interviews produced similar justifications. 'The crash convinced me that I was right not to buy shares. I thought I was right at the time and now I know. I know drivers, like myself, who have lost £500. That's a lot of money to lose in a day. With the building society at least your money is guaranteed' (Mr H, Basildon Conservative).

Summary

Share ownership is perhaps the clearest example of how the Conservatives have managed to confuse prosperity with political change. The spread of share ownership, like the spread of home ownership, is constantly trumpeted by ministers as if it signifies a personal endorsement of everything they do. In the case of share ownership, however, the increase in the number of shareholders from under 3 million to 9 million during the 1980s has not come about because 6 million people have been converted to the idea of 'popular capitalism', that widespread share ownership will make the economy stronger, but because they have been provided with a cash incentive to do so. As the October 1987 crash underlined, direct ownership of shares by individuals is not necessarily a good idea. It is certainly not as favoured by the tax system as one's principal private residence.

But since 1982 there has been a steep rise in the personal wealth of people in work. Not all of this has been soaked up in house prices and pensions, so when a straightforward chance to make a 25 per cent profit presents itself, there is a lot of spare cash around to take up the offer. Large numbers of small investors sold privatisation share offers immediately, but many of them kept them. Some of them don't know how to sell their shares, but in other cases it is inertia: the money may as well stay in shares if it is not needed for immediate spending.

The most important political function of the privatisation programme is to reward and reinforce the Conservatives' existing supporters. The evidence of opinion surveys and interviews is that Labour supporters are opportunistic about privatisation share issues, that most non-Labour supporters take a pragmatic view of state ownership and are ambivalent about share issues, and that only people who already believe in market forces are enthusiastic.

The non-ideological pragmatism of the majority echoes that of Clement Attlee, the Labour prime minister from 1945 to 1951, who had a perfectly undogmatic attitude to nationalisation even at its most popular according to a recent biographer. 'Attlee did not consider that nationalisation in itself was an integral part of socialism. It was one of several means to an end: control of the people's economy by the people and for the people' (Trevor Burridge, *Clement Attlee: A Political Biography*, p. 201).

8

Social Security

There's so many people taking money that they don't deserve and don't need, while genuine people are suffering all the time. The problem is people's greed. They're doing the genuine person out of money they really need.

Although most people can expect to be ill, have children and grow old, the majority go through their lives with little or no experience of unemployment. Even in November 1980, probably the most pessimistic point in the 1980–1 recession, two-thirds of those in work thought their jobs were safe, and three-quarters of the population said they or their families were not directly affected by unemployment (Gallup). Hence support for the National Health Service, schools and state pensions is bound to be somewhat different from that for social security. Because so many people have no direct self-interest in the state continuing to provide social security – indeed, as taxpayers, they have an interest in cutting benefits – attitudes towards social security are perhaps where a new individualism might be particularly expected.

Certainly, the Thatcher governments have not been generous with welfare payments, and this has been in tune with a feeling, widespread in 1979, that many social security claimants are scroungers. But attitudes to social security have changed, and, not surprisingly, people have become *less* likely to see claimants as scroungers and more likely to think that welfare benefits are too low.

In 1976, nearly half (43 per cent) of the British population thought that 'people who live in need' were poor mainly 'because of laziness or lack of willpower'. In 1983, only 22 per cent gave this reason, and three years later, 19 per cent did, with more people saying 'it's an inevitable part of modern life' (37 per cent) and citing 'injustice in our society' (25 per cent) as the main reasons for poverty. This shift in opinions took place at the same time as the numbers of the unemployed multiplied from 1.25 million in 1979 to 3 million in 1982.[1]

People in Britain became much less likely to blame the unemployed themselves for unemployment as a result of the recession of 1980–1. This seems logical: as the dole queues topped the 3 million mark it became impossible to argue that this was caused by a sharp increase in the number of lazy and shiftless workers.

But the government was not the main scapegoat, either; Gallup polls which offered respondents a different selection of scapegoats, reported that 'world economic pressures' (35 per cent) and trade unions (25 per cent) were more likely to be cited than the government (23 per cent) and 'people not wanting to work' (23 per cent) as 'the main cause' of unemployment, in June 1980, when the dole queues started snaking metaphorically through everyone's sitting room. This was still very different from 1977, when unemployment briefly touched 1.5 million and was thought to be a serious threat to civilisation as we know it; then its leading causes were thought to be trade unions (38 per cent) and 'people not wanting to work' (33 per cent). Things were *very* different then: even Margaret Thatcher was against unemployment in 1977. 'I think it's terrible if a person who wants to work cannot find a job. You have no self-respect, you haven't got the respect of your family, if somehow you cannot earn yourself a living and them a living too. Sometimes I have heard it said that the Conservatives have been associated with unemployment. That is absolutely wrong. We would have been drummed out of office if we'd had this level of unemployment' (Party political broadcast, 4 May 1977). Her tune, too, had changed by 1980. 'Unemployment may be [long pause] an unpalatable consequence of fighting inflation,' she told *The Sunday Times* (3 August 1980).

Nevertheless, her government managed to escape the blame. The high unemployment of the 1980s tends to be regarded fatalistically, as the fault neither of the government nor of the unemployed themselves. If letting the unemployed off the hook is logical, absolving the government is less rational, as even most classical economists now agree that the Conservatives' policy of high interest rates and the high pound in the dismal early years of Geoffrey Howe's Chancellorship, 1979–81, was at least 'overdone'. But these technical issues, of interest and exchange rates, 'monetarism' and supply-side economics, are quite indistinguishable from 'world economic pressures' to the person receiving the redundancy notice. The words are all jargon and the forces are all impersonal.

Regardless of whether job losses were the government's fault, however, the lack of blame attaching to many of the unemployed themselves caused a significant shift in attitudes towards welfare benefits between 1981 and 1987. The proportion of people thinking that the availability of welfare benefits had 'not gone far enough' went up from 33 per cent to 51 per cent; the proportion thinking it had 'gone too far' went down from 25 per cent to 16 per cent. Those saying it was 'about right' also went down from 36 to 26 per cent (Gallup).

All the same, the belief that large numbers of social security claimants are on the fiddle has persisted. Between 64 and 70 per cent of people agree that 'large numbers of people falsely claim benefits', according to the series of British Social Attitudes surveys since 1983 – that is, after the recession and the change in attitudes towards unemployment. But this is quite logical. If there were scroungers before, either in 'large numbers' or small ones, then the scroungers must still be there, down at the dole office, swindling the taxpayers out of millions. The fact that scroungers are now outnumbered (or more heavily outnumbered) by the deserving poor provides no better argument for indiscriminate generosity.

But, to peel off another layer of the onion of apparently contra-dictory public opinion, the belief in the existence of 'large numbers' of scroungers overlaps with an even stronger belief that there are 'large numbers of people who are elegible for benefits [but] fail to claim them' – between 79 and 84 per cent agree that this is the case.[2]

Gould Mattinson's post-election interviews show how these atti-tudes link in with the feeling of the fragility of prosperity among new Conservative voters in the 1987 election. While long-standing Conservatives felt hostile and unsympathetic towards social security claimants, new working-class Conservative voters had a more de-fensive or apolegetic attitude towards keeping their share of the cake. The difference was quite marked in attitudes towards the unemployed. 'You've got to look after your own first' (C1 Conserva-tive woman, ex-Labour). 'I know it's selfish, but that's the way the world is – it's dog eat dog' (C2 Conservative man, ex-Labour).

Convinced Conservatives tended to be harshly judgmental: 'I've seen programmes on television where there have been so-called poor people with a packet of fags and a video. She's right to be tough with them, they deserve it' (C2 always-Conservative man). But new Conservatives tended to generalise from their own experience and suggest that the poor should be as 'responsible' as themselves. 'People should look after themselves, it's just natural' (C2 ex-Labour woman).

Some ex-Labour voters feel that the problem of poverty has been exaggerated. 'I don't think there are as many poor people.' 'What are the Northerners moaning about?' 'I went away this year and I think I was the only one from south of Watford – everyone was from up North. They must be able to afford it.'

Most felt that, while the government should provide social security to those who have contributed in some way, it was not an automatic right. 'I've worked and deserve to have some back, but there are a lot of them claiming who haven't paid in and that's not fair' (C2 Conservative woman). This notion of contributory benefits, of course, lay behind the National Insurance scheme as it was originally conceived by William Beveridge in 1944. (People still have a strong sense of paying their 'stamp' – although they very often think the benefits include the National Health Service, which is actually funded out of general taxation.) This is connected with attitudes to taxation – if people could be sure extra taxes would get through to extra services for themselves, they would gladly pay (see p. 126).

There is a danger, however, in becoming overwhelmed by 'scroungerphobia' and forgetting the other half of the picture: that there are very high levels of support across the political spectrum for state benefits for the 'genuinely' unemployed. Our interviews found that this support for welfare benefits was strongly stated, although equally strongly qualified.

'If there is a lack of employment in their particular trade or a lack of work in their area, then fair enough, the government should help them' (Mr B, non-voter, skilled manual worker). 'The people who really are unemployed, like the redundant shipworker, should be given a decent income. But not the window cleaner who signs on' (Ms D, Conservative, personal assistant). 'I suppose they've got to [give the unemployed a decent income], or they wouldn't have anything to live on. Benefits are enough to live on; they just have to live within the money they're given. Although I'm sure many of them earn money on the side and don't declare it' (Ms J, Alliance, library assistant). 'There is a lot of people that need help, I think. But there's so many people taking money that they don't deserve and don't need, like in the black economy, while genuine people are suffering all the time. The problem is people's greed. They're doing the genuine person out of money they really need' (Hugh, Conservative electrician who last voted Labour in 1979).

Experience of the system only seems to reinforce belief in widespread fiddling. 'I do think the unemployed should be given a decent unemployment benefit. I don't hold with spongers. Having had the experience of visiting an unemployment exchange earlier this year I think the system stinks. But the hangers-on are terrible' (Mr E, Conservative, bank clerk). 'Last year I was in hospital and I couldn't work for three months. I'm buying my own place, and I got absolutely no help off the NHS [DHSS]: all I got was I think just under £30 a week. If I hadn't had my own insurance, God knows what would have happened. Yet I know people that are getting new fridges and beds for their children and that, and they're on the dole doing nothing at all. Well, they're not doing nothing, because some of them are motor mechanics. Doing jobs on the side' (Jack, Conservative, self-employed carpet-fitter).

Unlike Gould Mattinson's interviews, there was no mention in our interviews of the contributory principle – on the contrary, the clear implication was generally that, provided strict conditions were met, there should be a non-contributory 'basic income' for the genuine unemployed. A willingness to provide properly for those deemed to be in real need was balanced – some might say overshadowed – by a willingness to be authoritarian with the undeserving. The idea of forcing lazy people to work for benefits was not uncommon. 'Yes [they should have a decent income], 'if they're not lazy and pack the job in. If they do that then they should wait a lot longer then they now have to to claim benefit. If they've been sacked then they should get a certain amount. But rather than let them stay on the dole for years on end, there must be lots of jobs they can do in the community,' said Mr H, Conservative (last voted Labour in 1979), lorry driver.

'In some cases, yes. In places where there are no jobs they shouldn't be scrimping and scraping to bring their children up in a decent way. But those who are just lazy should be offered alternative employment and if they don't wish to take it they should be chucked off the dole,' said Ms F, Conservative in 1987, but now would vote Labour, unemployed and looking after the home.

'State benefits are a duty. They should be paid for a certain period anyway. And they should be made to work for it. They shouldn't be allowed to spend it on beer and fags. That's just a waste. They should be given vouchers for food and the rent and that,' said Mr P, an ardent Conservative and semi-skilled manual worker who said he had never felt threatened by unemployment.

'Yes,' said Mr A in Putney, it should be the government's duty to provide a decent income for the unemployed. His own work situation was highly insecure. 'You just never know when you might be out of a job. You could be out of work any time. I feel threatened by unemployment all the time. When it was first on the cards five years ago I used to worry, but not now. It's mainly just a tactic used by management to get the deals they want.' But this didn't soften his attitude to scroungers. 'You have to be careful because there are an awful lot of people who don't want to work' (voted Alliance in 1987, although feels closer to Labour).

Of course, the threat or the fact of unemployment does not have a mechanical relationship with political beliefs. Mr L in Wolverhampton, who switched from Labour to the Tories in the 1987 election, had been made redundant four days before our interview – on Christmas Eve (some employers are all heart). But he still regarded voting Tory as being in his 'best interests'.

Apart from Mr A, who didn't have children, and Mr L, who had rather more immediate problems of his own, most of our interviewees were concerned much more about their children's job prospects. Mr B, a non-voter who nevertheless thought of himself as being closer to the Labour Party than any other, and a skilled manual worker, said: 'I don't have any fears for myself but I do worry about the children's future. It seems as if there will be less work to go around. Obviously I'm concerned, but you don't know what's going to happen tomorrow, let alone in ten years' time. You can only live day by day and get their education right so they have a decent chance in life.'

The fear of unemployment was often seen in terms of society as a whole changing, with new technology changing the nature and amount of work, and social change affecting the geography of work. 'I live with the fear of unemployment. For my children, yes I do worry. Obviously there are going to be less jobs around because of technology' (Mr D, Conservative, self-employed painter-decorator).

'I think my children are threatened by unemployment. The old days, when you could say "my father was an engine driver so I'm going to be one" are gone. Times are moving fast' (Mr E, quite long-standing Conservative, bank clerk).

The 'you've got to move with the times' sentiment enables people in the South to categorise those in the North not as outright scroungers, but as unwilling to face up to change. No one mentioned Norman Tebbit's bicycle, but its after-image is there somewhere, being pedalled hard.

'There are jobs around for those who want them. The unemployed in the North should try and move down South, where there is plenty of work. When I was unemployed I didn't have enough to live on. And the benefit office doesn't tell you what you're entitled to. You only get what you ask for' (Mr G, Conservative, skilled manual worker).

'There is a difference between those who are unemployed and the unemployable. I think they should start to make a distinction between those people who are unemployable because there isn't any work for them and the unemployed who could find work if they wanted to. If you look in papers like the *Evening Standard* you can see thousands of job vacancies. If you're in a mining town and the only industry closes down then they should be paid benefit. And they should be helped with retraining and relocating. If they don't want to move then it's a more difficult question. I don't think anyone can say they don't want to move any more,' said Mr D, the Conservative self-employed painter-decorator. But this is still a long way from Tebbit's crudity.

The need to move with the times provides an extra sharp edge to aspirations for their children's education. 'I worry about the children's future,' said Mr H, a lorry driver who voted Conservative in 1987 (last voted Labour in 1979). 'We encourage their education. The boy's got a computer. The key is a good education; I don't want him to miss out like I did. He will learn because without Maths and good English he'll not be able to get a job anywhere.'

It is not just a question of their children 'getting on' or 'not missing out like I did', but in some cases of simply surviving in a more hostile labour market. 'I worry about my daughter and that's why I've kept her on at school' (Ms F, Conservative in 1987 but now Labour, unemployed and looking after the home). 'My boys are lucky because they were specifically trained for the jobs they do on London Transport. The cutbacks didn't really affect them' (Ms J, Alliance, library assistant).

Only one of our interviewees was unconcerned about unemployment and confident about the future of the economy. Ms D, a personal assistant who votes Conservative, said: 'I don't feel threatened by unemployment. For my son, it depends which area he wants to go into. Traditional jobs go but new jobs take their place.'

And only two said, unprompted, that they saw unemployment as a threat to the country as a whole. 'I don't feel threatened. But I feel unemployment in general is a threat to a society. I can only see the figure getting worse. I don't feel it will threaten the nation, GB Ltd – that will probably carry on being very profitable for some people. But for the whole of the people it's a different matter,' said Mr K, a wages clerk who didn't vote in 1987 and who thought 'the level of benefit could probably be a bit higher'.

And the government should provide the unemployed with a decent income, said Mr N, 'for social reasons. If you don't, you're going to have anarchy. [Unemployment] is still a worry. I'm not worried personally, we're doing very well as a company. But it'll take a long time before we [the country] are back like it was ten years ago' (SDP in 1987, engineering supervisor).

Explaining attitudes to social security

One of the important – but unpublicised – findings of the group of researchers working on the British Election Studies and British Social Attitudes series is that attitudes to social security have more to do with ideas of discipline than they do with questions of material equality. What this means is that people who think that there is too big a gap between rich and poor are not especially likely to support generous welfare benefits for the poor, which would be one obvious way of trying to close the gap. Supporters of benefits in fact tend to be people who are liberal on questions of law and order, regardless of whether they think society is too unequal.

Hidden away in an 'end of award' report (a technical report saying what they have spent their grant on) to the Economic and Social Research Council, are the results of a special exercise designed to improve the questionnaires for the British Election Studies and British Social Attitudes surveys.[3] The researchers tried out new questions and tested how consistent the answers were and how closely related answers were to each other. One of the sets of new questions was a batch concerning social security. They found that the people who gave 'right-wing' answers to these questions also tended to give 'right-wing' answers to another batch of questions about law and order, which they use to measure people's position on a 'liberal versus authoritarian' scale. But the same people did not give consistently 'right-wing' answers to a third batch of questions about equality.

The set of questions on social security asked whether respondents agreed or disagreed with these statements:

Social security

Many people who get social security don't really deserve any help.

The welfare state makes people less willing to look after themselves.

If welfare benefits weren't so generous people would learn to stand on their own two feet.

The government should [not] spend more money on welfare benefits.

Most people on the dole are fiddling in one way or another.

People who gave 'illiberal' or 'right-wing' answers (that is, they agreed with the statements) to these questions were likely to do so consistently, both within the group of questions and if they were asked them again. Another computer analysis showed that the same people were also likely to agree with three similar questions not included in the batch: 'When someone is unemployed it's usually his or her own fault'; 'Too many people these days like to rely on government handouts'; and 'If a person really wants a job he [sic] can usually find one.'

116

But more importantly they were also likely to give 'illiberal' or 'right-wing' answers to questions about law and order, the liberal-versus-authoritarian batch. These included:

Authority

Young people today don't have enough respect for traditional British values.

Schools should teach children to obey authority.

The law should always be obeyed even if a particular law is wrong.

Censorship of films and magazines is necessary to uphold moral standards.

People who break the law should be given stiffer sentences.

But what political scientists think of as 'right wing' in these matters is not closely related in most people's minds with what political scientists think of as 'right wing' in economics. The people who gave 'illiberal' replies to the questions on social security and authority were not significantly likely to give anti-egalitarian replies to a batch of questions about equality. These questions about equality had been specifically chosen as a 'left wing versus right wing' batch because they were the ones that most sharply separated Labour and Conservative supporters.

Equality

Government should redistribute income from the better off to those who are less well off.

Big business benefits owners at the expense of workers.

Ordinary working people do not get their fair share of the nation's wealth.

There is one law for the rich and one for the poor.

Management will always try to get the better of employees if it gets the chance.

The responses to these five statements were more consistent than the results obtained by asking people to place themselves on a scale marked 'left' to 'right'. In in-depth follow-up interviews to assess the reliability of the left–right scales, the researchers found that 8 per cent of respondents said they didn't know what left or right meant, while another third of their sample gave a 'wrong' answer, or rather gave an answer which did not 'correspond closely to the political scientists' concept' (such as describing the left as people who are extreme, dogmatic or militant, but without saying what they are extreme, dogmatic or militant *about*; or describing the right as moderate, middle of the road, centrist, Labour or communist).[4]

The researchers' main finding – that hostility towards welfare benefits is more closely related to authoritarian attitudes than to anti-egalitarian ones – may seem surprising, but it is logical. The belief in 'large numbers' of scroungers is a moral, not an economic, one. And *if* there are a lot of scroungers, then universal social security benefits are not a good way of providing for those genuinely in need, even if, as most of our interviewees did, people want to see the poor provided for and the gap between rich and poor narrowed. Hence the worry in our interviews about people being 'lazy' and the need for them to be 'made to work'.

If the three collections of statements are examined more closely, the ones about social security are in fact statements of social morality, and not directly about economic equality. Our interviews show that support for social security (on egalitarian grounds) is there, but is overlaid by concern about abuse of the system.

This reinforces the argument that egalitarianism has often been misinterpreted in surveys like British Social Attitudes. Where the less well-off see redistribution as benefiting them, they support it – but they are often more interested in the benefit rather than in the principle of equality.

Furthermore, the statements about equality in the cluster on p. 117 are closely related to class and the idea of a society divided along class lines: working-class people are likely to endorse 'equality' on the grounds that they resent class divisions rather than differences of income or wealth as such. The statements assume a society made up of two classes (better off/less well off, owners/workers, rich/poor, management/employees) which ignores security claimants. Working-class people are willing on self-interested grounds to support the interests of their class against the better off, the owners, the rich or the management, but do not necessarily support the interests of social security claimants if they see them as clashing with those of the rest of the working class. Belief in 'large numbers' of scroungers puts a block between those in and out of work and denies that their interests could be the same.

Summary

The fear of unemployment made it the 'most important problem facing the country' when people were interviewed by opinion poll-sters in 1980–1; at the end of 1981 the Conservatives were trailing third in the opinion polls and Mrs Thatcher was the most unpopular prime minister since the start of opinion polling.[5] Unemployment went on being cited as the 'most important problem' until the state of the NHS supervened in the spring of 1988, but the fear went out of it as soon as the recession bottomed out and real earnings for those remaining in work started to rise sharply in 1982. As a result, as Peter Jenkins astutely observed: 'Unemployment had been redefined in people's minds as a social problem rather than as an economic indicator.'[6]

This explains the puzzle of why the Conservatives have been able to win two elections with unemployment standing at over 3 million. The state of the economy is the most powerful factor affecting short-term electoral performance, and the huge importance of the rate of unemployment used to be because it indicated how well the whole economy was doing. The 'unbalanced recovery' since 1982 has broken the link between most people's prosperity and the rate of unemployment, and so, although unemployment is still seen as a major problem, its significance has reversed. It has become a test of altruism instead of an indicator of personal well-being.

Because of the 'informed fatalism' of Marshall *et al.* (*Social Class in Modern Britain*, p. 156), the altruism of the British electorate is limited to situations where they can be sure the unfortunate will benefit from it. They conclude that their sample

would endorse such redistributive efforts as were likely to result in a more just society, but judge these unlikely to be forthcoming given existing social, economic and political arrangements. They do not approve of social injustice, can conceive both of a more just society and the means by which it might be achieved, but nevertheless have judged present arrangements to be largely unassailable. Under these circumstances a self-interested and pragmatic collectivism is perfectly rational. (p. 157)

This altruism rests on a slope: it can slide away from the apparent egalitarianism which forms part of the case for saying that Thatcherism has no hold on the popular mood – into the authoritarian attitudes which are really at the heart of the modern Conservative appeal. In Chapter 10 the analysis of the connection between morality and individualism is taken further, based on in-depth discussions with two groups of working-class people in South London.

The key to attitudes towards social security is the idea of 'the scrounger', one which inhabits the moral universe rather than the world of economics. To the extent that people have become more sympathetic to the plight of the unemployed during the Thatcher years, people have become less individualistic. But underlying beliefs haven't changed, and now that unemployment has been falling steadily since the autumn of 1986, the spectre of the scrounger may rise again and sympathy for the unemployed fall off.

9

Prosperity

Money doesn't make people think any different, does it, really? Everybody's got a conscience. Or most people have.

After Labour's third election defeat in a row, the party's leader faced its annual conference and demanded that policy should be thoroughly reviewed to meet the challenges of the time: 'The changing character of labour, full employment, new housing, the new way of living based on the telly, the fridge, the car and glossy magazines – all these have an effect on our political strength.' The reference to full employment and the fridge give it away. It wasn't Neil Kinnock, it was Hugh Gaitskell in 1959. But otherwise it could have been said after the 1987 election.

Thirty years after Harold Macmillan declared that 'most of our people have never had it so good', the Labour Party was again afraid that prosperity was eroding the loyalty to it of the working class. Then, as now, Labour voters were acquiring consumer durables and the government was declaring: 'We've never had it so good for the 87 per cent of us who are working' (Lord Young, 1986).

Gaitskell's fridge should be a warning against a fear of prosperity. If someone now suggested that owning fridges makes people vote Tory, much amusement would be had, and jokes would no doubt be made about their being one cube short of a full tray in the ice box.

But some people in the Labour Party are still afraid that if the working classes own houses, shares, microwave ovens or a timeshare in a 'little place in Marbella', they won't vote Labour any more. 'The cult of individual affluence emphasised values of selfishness, greed and materialism [and was] fostered by a revitalised Tory party and the mass media, especially commercial television. Visions of a fairyland with a cornucopia of consumer goods for all individuals had great popular appeal. The mass market society pushed collectivism to one side.' So wrote Eric Deakins, former MP for Walthamstow, in 1988 (*What Future for Labour?* p. 8). His book is a classic of the 'Fear of Fridges' school of thought. Its title is an echo of a famous Penguin book published in 1960, *Must Labour Lose?*, which concluded that it wasn't inevitable, but winning was fast becoming impossible because the working class was shrinking, and getting richer.

But just as the fridge effect was nonsense in 1959, the fridge-freezer effect was nonsense in 1987. As was demonstrated in Chapters 4 and 7, there is no evidence that governments *can* buy ideological loyalty. Rising living standards can make some people vote Tory once or twice. But they do not change people's basic values from cooperation to competition. Despite strongly rising real after-tax incomes for those in work between 1983 and 1987, the Conservative vote fell by 0.1 percentage points in successive General Elections.

Deakins announced that 'a new set of dominant values [has] emerged'. But there is no evidence that it has. Of course, the overwhelming majority of people who are working, whether working class or middle class, are substantially better off than they have ever been. They indeed live in a 'fairyland with a cornucopia of consumer goods', but are people *more* acquisitive than they used to be, or do they just have more acquisitions? The consumer trends towards green and ethical products point in the opposite direction.

Perhaps it is not surprising that Deakins should have fallen victim to the fridge fallacy; not only has he always been a dedicated anti-materialist (in his book he attacks Britain's 'addiction to economic growth', and in his first speech in the Commons in 1970 he said that drug-taking was a rejection of materialism), but he was also one of the three Labour MPs – all in London – to lose their seats in the 1987 election. The performance of the economy is the strongest short-term factor affecting the way people vote. And it is true that the South and East, and parts of London in particular, have done very well under Mrs Thatcher and have voted accordingly. But this doesn't mean that people have been converted to her values of individualism, private provision and free-market economics – not even in the South-East.

The parallels between 1959 and 1987 are not exact, but they are nevertheless striking. And the deleterious effect of prosperity on Labour voting was debunked last time. *The Affluent Worker* in 1968 tested the thesis of the 'embourgeoisement' of the working class by surveying car workers in the 1960s boom town of Luton. 'Our findings are certainly not what would have been expected, following the argument which links the achievement of affluence with increasing working-class conservatism,' concluded its authors. 'Rather, they are in line with the results of studies made in other advanced societies which also indicate that manual workers can attain relatively high standards of living and still remain strong adherents of left-wing or labour-oriented parties' (p. 172).

In 1987, the Labour Party leadership was a little wiser: it realised that prosperity may make people vote Conservative without actually making them Conservatives, but it recognised that the party failed to get the right message across. This is the significance of the little parable first told by transport union leader Ron Todd after the General Election. The parable concerned a docker earning £400 a week, who owned £500-worth of British Gas shares and had bought his own council house, and a little place in Marbella. According to Todd, you do not say to such a person: 'Let me take you out of your misery, brother.' Neil Kinnock thought it such a good line that he used it in his speech to the Labour Party conference in Brighton that October. Neither Todd nor Kinnock, unlike Gaitskell, see affluence as an obstacle to socialism (although it should be pointed out that a minuscule proportion of manual workers are *that* affluent – only 1.3 per cent of male manual workers earn £400 a week or more).[1] And they are right; the style of collectivism may change as people become better off, but the principle remains the same.

Most of the former Labour voters in our discussion groups thought that winning the pools would be likely to make people more selfish, but went on to say they would actually be more generous themselves. With the women, this generosity was limited to their own family. Janet said: 'I'd be more generous with my own. I'd make sure they all had what they wanted, and were secure.' Wendy said: 'I'd be more generous to the family and friends and relations.'

The men, on the other hand, were more likely to say they would be generous beyond their family. Hugh said: 'I think you would give some money away.' David pointed out: 'We give money now and we're not that rich.' Jonathan said: 'If you were used to poor times and then you've suddenly got a lot of money, then you would.' Jack went on: 'But anybody that's born to money just doesn't know what being poor means. To them the headlines in the papers about an old woman mugged and that doesn't mean anything at all.' Tony said: 'Oh, I think it would. Doesn't matter how much money anybody's got, when they see headlines about old age pensioners being mugged and that, it must make them think what terrible things are happening. Money doesn't make people think any different, does it, really? Everybody's got a conscience. Or most people have.'

Tax cuts or collective services?

If increasing prosperity did have the effect of changing people's values, then the Conservative policy of income tax cuts should not only win electoral support, but should also win ideological support for the value of individualism, the idea that people should provide for themselves rather than pay taxes to the state to provide for everyone. The Conservatives have succeeded on the first count but not on the second. Most voters who switched from Labour in 1987 felt that the economy was doing well and saw themselves benefiting from Conservative tax cuts, according to Gould Mattinson's post-election inquest. 'I think that life will improve with taxes going down' (C1 Conservative woman). 'If you're self-employed like me you're a lot better off by tax concessions' (C1 Conservative man). 'I think we've all got used to a higher standard of living. You expect to have certain things these days' (C1 Conservative man).

But on the principle of whether lower taxes are more desirable than better services, the Conservatives have lost the argument comprehensively. Gallup has asked people which they prefer throughout the Thatcher years, and there has been a dramatic shift from individualism to collectivism. Gallup asked: 'People have different views about whether it is more important to reduce taxes or keep up government spending. Which of these statements comes closest to your own view?'

Taxes being cut, even if it means some reduction in government services, such as health, education and welfare.

Things should be left as they are.

Government services such as health, education and welfare should be extended, even if it means some increases in taxes.[2]

	Mar 1979	Feb 1983	Feb 1985	Sept 1986	May 1987	Oct 1987
	%	%	%	%	%	%
Tax cuts	34	23	16	9	12	11
Better services	34	49	59	68	61	66

Of course, this shift is explained by the fact that people feel that services like the NHS and schools have been underfunded if not actually cut back since 1979, and that taxes have been cut, so people now feel that the balance should now go the other way. But if tax cuts were winning ideological support, more than one person in ten would be expected to back the individualist option.

Wait a minute, say some of the more cynical members of the 'Fear of Fridges' school of thought. If 61 per cent of the voters wanted higher taxes and better services in the month before the 1987 General Election, why didn't they vote for them? Why did Labour get in such a mess over its taxation policy, which involved higher taxes for an indeterminate number of people? Surely the electorate is saying one thing to the pollsters and then, in the privacy of the polling booth, voting selfishly for quite another?

In the run-up to the 1987 election, Harris Research did indeed discover that electors had different priorities that weren't normally picked up by opinion polls. Harris looked for an explanation for why the Conservatives were in the lead in the opinion polls despite the fact that the voters thought that unemployment was the most important problem facing the country, and that Labour had the best policies to deal with it. Instead of asking 'what are the most important problems facing the country?' Harris rephrased the question to ask 'what are the most important issues facing you and your family?' And substantially fewer people thought that unemployment was an important issue for them and their family.

But this doesn't actually mean that voters are secretly more selfish than they usually let on. It is not surprising that more people think unemployment is a national problem than are affected by it personally. Nor does it explain Labour's failure to obtain more votes. In fact, rephrasing the question ought to have operated in Labour's favour. True, unemployment becomes less important. But so does defence, a strong Tory issue. And the NHS becomes the most important issue, while other 'Labour' issues, education and pensions, also become more important. The only 'Tory' issues to become more important are well down the list: law and order, and taxation.[3]

Table 2 The two most important problems

	Facing the country %	Facing you and your family %
Unemployment	49	39
Defence	35	16
NHS	33	42
Education	19	24
Pensions	10	14
Law and order	6	16
Taxation	6	13

One reason why the importance attached to 'pro-Labour' issues didn't translate into Labour votes was because Labour's policies of higher spending, for example on health and education, are not primarily supported out of altruism but out of collective self-interest. And, as Gould Mattinson discovered, the reluctance of Labour defectors to contribute in practice to collective services is often explained by a worry about whether they would personally benefit from them, or whether the money would go to the 'right' place. 'Only if I had the proof it was going there, and I was getting something back' (C2 Conservative woman). 'If I really believed that it would go to services – but I don't think it would' (C1 Alliance woman). 'I'd pay more if I thought I was going to get it, but it doesn't get back to where you want it' (Ex-Labour woman).

On the other hand, tax cuts have had less of an impact than Conservative propaganda would imply. 'Tax cuts haven't really made a lot of difference because it's only a few extra pounds each week. I'd like to be better off, but that will only happen if we work harder. I also think the economy will get better and that will help,' said Ms D, a Putney Conservative. 'Tax cuts under Thatcher haven't really helped because you're really only talking about a couple of extra pounds a week,' said Mr A, an Alliance voter.

These comments are perhaps not surprising, given the Tories' real record on taxation, which is to have increased the total tax burden (including VAT and National Insurance contributions) to record peacetime levels (see p. 99). Even in the 1988 Budget, which brought the top rate of income tax down from 60 to 40 per cent, Nigel Lawson candidly admitted that 'it will not be possible in this Budget to reduce the burden of taxation – that is to say, to reduce taxation as a share of GDP [national income]'. In which case, the 95 per cent of taxpayers who are *not* in the higher-rate bracket were, by his own admission, shouldering a relatively greater tax burden.

The sensitivity of the taxation issue for Labour at the last election lay in the fragility of the prosperity that the better-off of the working class have enjoyed. The danger that Labour might increase taxes was felt to be far more pressing than the positive attraction of the Conservatives continuing to pare the occasional tuppence off the basic rate of income tax. Deborah Mattinson summed up the attitudes of working-class new Conservatives thus: 'They consider themselves to be better off in most aspects of their lives, but this feeling of wellbeing is fragile and vulnerable, resulting in an apparently harsh "I'm all right, Jack" philosophy.'

This sense of insecurity was often associated with the idea, held especially by Tory women, that the economy was static, in the sense that to pay for something you have to take it from something else. One C2 Conservative woman commented: 'If they [the government] create jobs something else has got to suffer for it.' 'Can't work it any other way,' agreed another. 'The money's got to come from somewhere.'

Mr D, a self-employed Labour-to-Conservative defector in 1987, said: 'I am better off because I've worked harder. Every year I have to work harder whether I like it or not. [The future] really depends on my own efforts, it has nothing to do with the general economic outlook. Even if the economy was going through a bad stage I'd just have to make a bigger effort.'

However, while values may not have changed, the Tories have quite successfully worked 'ownership' and 'being better off' into their rhetoric, while the opposition parties have failed to counter them. This was recognised by Ron Todd and Neil Kinnock after the election, but they still have a long way to go in convincing the electorate that the Labour Party wants people to succeed and get on and become better off.

In our discussion groups Ann, a home help who switched to the Conservatives in 1987, said: 'I think the Conservatives are more for people to get on, if they can. But, not being in the position of being out of work and being short of money, it doesn't really affect me, but if I was, then I should think I would be against the Conservatives.' And Di, a librarian, agreed: 'Certainly in the last maybe ten years they have prompted people to take chances and go out on their own and buy their own properties, and things like that which weren't there before.'

This has enabled the Conservatives to take full advantage of the fact that rising living standards always benefit the party in government. At the same time, however, the benefits of the economic recovery since 1982 have been unusually restricted to certain groups of people and certain parts of the country. In June 1985 only 22 per cent of people said that 'people like themselves' were better off than when the Conservatives came to power; and in the autumn of 1987 and spring of 1988 only 27 per cent of people said that their households' financial situation had got better in the previous year.[4] People who do not feel that they are better off are much less likely to vote Conservative. Most of our interviewees who said they were worse off than they were five years ago were non-Tories. Mr B, a Labour-inclined non-voter in 1987 and a skilled manual worker, said:

> Financially I'm worse off. I'm in a job that gives a yearly increase that is supposed to be equivalent to the rate of the increase in the cost of living. But the real cost of the standard of living has been rising faster than my wage increase. The government is, or seems to be, encouraging private health systems, running down the NHS, and education is coming to the stage where if you have the money to pay for it you can have it but if you haven't you're losing out. So in many ways you have to find more money just to stay the same.

Ms C, a Labour-voting pensioner, was equally unimpressed by claims of a booming economy:

I don't think we will be better off, we'll probably be worse off. It all depends on this government. We already have to pay for teeth and spectacles and she doesn't seem to know where to get the money from next. Even if the economy improves we won't notice any difference. They say we're doing well now, okay, but why aren't all the people of this country working? Why aren't there more houses? When you think of all those people sleeping rough, under arches, it's incredible, it's never been known before.

The class divide remains

This identification of material advancement with the Tories is neither inevitable nor evidence that individualist values are spreading. While it is true, as Eric Deakins says, that 'visions of a fairyland with a cornucopia of consumer goods for all individuals [have] great popular appeal', his corollary does not follow. He argues that 'constant improvements in living standards weakened political resolve to change the economic system for a better one [and] made people less likely to accept their share of social responsibility for others who had not done so well.'

It seems plausible, but it isn't true. The 1930s were the last time when the British economic system was incapable of providing subsistence for large numbers of people. Since then, the unfairness of the economic system has decreased but is now increasing. Real incomes in general have risen since 1979, or since 1982 at least (although not for many people dependent on social security benefits), but the inequality of incomes has increased sharply since 1979. The share of the richest tenth of the population has grown at the expense of that of the poorer half.[5] And, although there has been a continuing expansion of middle-class employment, the relative chances of people from different class backgrounds getting good jobs have not changed. Class inequalities in access to sixth-form and university education have similarly stayed the same.[6]

The relative gap between the working and middle classes, then, has not changed. But has consumerism affected the way people see material divisions in society? There is no evidence that it has. Support for the collectivist role of the state in 'redistributing income and wealth towards ordinary working people' has been unchanged at an average of 52 per cent since at least 1974; and as many as seven out of ten people agree with the slightly more anodyne statement that it should be 'the government's responsibility to reduce income differences between rich and poor' (see p. 33).

Our interviews found that most new Conservatives agreed with this mild egalitarianism, and saw society as unequal. Mr E, a Conservative clerk who last voted Labour in 1974, agreed that it was the government's responsibility to reduce income differences between rich and poor and said: 'We are not born equal, some of us are better endowed than others.'

The question was seen almost exclusively in terms of tax policy, rather than as a question about welfare benefits or job creation. Ms F, a Conservative voter in 1987, who last voted Labour in 1983 and who intends to revert in future, said: 'At the moment, the poor are taxed more than the rich and the situation will be even worse once the poll tax is introduced.' Mr H, a Conservative lorry driver who last voted Labour in 1979, said: 'It's only fair that the better off should pay more taxes.' Mr L, an unskilled manual worker who switched from Labour to Conservative in 1987, said: 'They never take much off them, the rich, do they?' Ms L, who switched from Labour to Conservative in 1987, said: 'I think we should all be on the same level. They should all be on the same level, like these Japanese, they do all the same work and that, and I think we should be the same.'

Even Mr T, a skilled fitter and lifelong Conservative voter, said: 'I do, definitely. It seems as though they [the Conservatives] are just looking after their own. I know I said I vote Conservative, but they seem to think that below their own class there's no one else.'

Ms D, a personal assistant who switched from Labour to Conservative in 1983, was the most ambivalent, saying: 'It wouldn't be fair to take money away from people if they've worked hard for it, but in an ideal world it would be nice to share the money of the rich around so that everyone had a little more.'

Only a minority of new Conservatives, and one Liberal, disagreed with the government doing something to narrow the income gap. Mr D, a self-employed switcher from Labour to Conservative in 1987, said: 'If you want a better way of life for yourself it's up to you. You can't expect governments to do it for you. There are plenty of opportunities for everyone.' Mr G, a Conservative machine operator, said: 'People who earn a good wage should not be taxed as heavily as they are.' Mr Q, a Conservative voter who last voted Labour in 1974, was a little doubtful: 'If people are rich they usually deserve it. I know there are some that don't but if you work hard you should keep it.' And Ms O, mature law student who switched from Labour to Liberal in 1987, said: 'Not really. Everyone has their own job, and what they get for it is up to them.'

Apart from these 'individualists', however, there was no difference between the Conservatives and our Labour, Alliance or floating voters, who overwhelmingly favoured redistribution. Mr A, who voted Alliance in 1987 but would now vote Labour, said: 'The only people who benefit from tax cuts are the wealthy and they are the people who least need the extra money.' Mr C, a retired supervisor, undecided between Labour and Alliance, said: 'Too many of these big people get large sums of money too easily.' Ms E, an Alliance voter who last voted Labour in 1974, said: 'You can't expect people on a low salary to pay the same rate of taxation as those on a high wage.'

Mr K, a non-voting clerk who thinks of himself as closer to Labour, said: 'No one else except the government can redistribute wealth, you certainly can't leave the job to the business community. Free enterprise is a good thing but it can't be left unchecked, it has to be reined in.' Ms J, a library assistant and an Alliance voter since 1966, said: 'I think there is too wide a gap between those who have and those who have nothing.' Mr N, an engineering supervisor who voted SDP in 1987 and who had voted Labour in the past, said: 'There should be differences in income, it's just that there shouldn't be any poor. It is the government's responsibility to arrange it so there aren't poor people.'

Only Mr B, a non-voting skilled machinist who thought of himself as being closer to Labour, took a 'hard' egalitarian line, saying: 'Overpaid people should have their wages cut by the government. People should be paid a fair rate for the job they do.'

The class divide remains, even if some don't think it has widened; more importantly, most of our interviewees thought it was just as hard or harder for them to cross it as it had always been. At a personal level, most people simply do not recognise that 'opportunities' in life have been widened by the Conservative government, even if they believe that Britain in general is forging ahead. This is because there is a contradiction between rising living standards, which most of our interviewees enjoy, and the fact that their standing *relative* to the middle class, the 'upper crust', the 'high fliers', hasn't changed in the past decade. Class antagonisms are alive and well in Britain today. Take, for example, Mr G's embittered comment about his former employers: 'I was unemployed for three years. During that time I was very badly off. I was made redundant from a maintenance job. I blame the company for that, it had nothing to do with the economy. It was the upper-crust management, who think they know everything but they don't. They seemed to be changing offices every day of the week, just because the director didn't like the colour scheme.'

It might not seem necessary to point out that class divisions have become deeper and sharper in a period which has included the 1984–5 miners' strike and a more unequal distribution of income than at any time since the war. But this is exactly what the Fear of Fridges school of thought appears to deny. The idea that parts of the working class have been made permanently bourgeois by prosperity does imply that class antagonisms have been softened, because we are 'all middle class now'. (Mrs Thatcher puts it the other way round: 'We are all working people, who basically want the same things.')[7] The truth is that as some working-class people attain 'middle-class' standards of living, they find that the middle classes are already as far above them on the ladder of income and wealth as they were before.

We asked our interviewees whether they thought 'getting to the top' in Britain was easier today than ten years ago. The non-Tories were most likely to think it had got harder. But two Conservatives didn't think it had become any easier to get to the top. Mr E, who last voted Labour in 1970 or 1974, thought there had been no change in the past ten years: 'There was a time when I believed you could go from the bottom to the top but really it's a closed shop up there. You've got the public schools and anyone outside of that background is never permitted to join. It's always been the same and that hasn't altered one jot.'

Mr H, a lorry driver who last voted Labour in 1979, was also sceptical about the idea of greater social mobility: 'I wouldn't know if it has improved throughout the country but I know that within my company it's very easy to climb the ladder. There are several managers above me who were former drivers. [But] I don't think the image of American-style success touches ordinary people. You hear about the yuppies in the City making vast amounts of money and dashing around in Porsches but that's really only for them.'

The only Conservative voter in 1987 to say that it had actually become harder to get to the top was Mr L, who voted Labour in 1983: 'Hard. Ten years ago, you could give up a job and go into another one, straight away, but now there's more obstacles. I think it's harder now.'

And even those new Conservatives who believed that it had become easier for working-class people to make it to the top by individual effort still emphasised the barriers. Mr P, an aggressive Thatcherite, said: 'It's never been easy. The Conservatives like to keep them [the rich] there, but they want to give everybody else a chance too. She makes it easier for people to better themselves – you get rewarded if you work hard. [But] no matter how much of a Christian you are, there's always going to be them up there and the rest down here, but they're interested in allowing more people to make it to the top.'

Mr D, who switched from Labour to the Conservatives in 1987, said: 'Chances for working-class people have improved, providing they want to work for it. You hear about people who have suddenly been slung out of a job after years with the same company – they find that they really have to do something for themselves so they find something they really want to do and like doing and make a go of it. That's half the battle really, finding something you enjoy working at. It may be hard going at first but if you want it hard enough you will get it.' But then he went on: 'The eighties is totally different from the sixties when it seemed as if all the working class were doing well for themselves. Everybody seemed to have loads of money in the sixties, there was loads of work about and I was working all the time doing all sorts of things. I didn't have to worry so much.'

His wife, who last voted Labour in 1979, referred back not to the sixties but to her father's generation, in comparison with which the Thatcher Era was an unqualified bonus:

I do think there are more opportunities for everyone. The growth in small businesses is one example of this. I think it's marvellous that more people have been given a chance to start their own businesses. My parents would never have had that in their day. If my father had been given the chance of a bank loan or government grant he would have been a very good businessman. Success is encouraged under Thatcher and because she has been around for a long time now everyone seems to want to be successful – maybe we've been brainwashed. You find it in sports. Ten years ago British people were happy to say you did well if you came second but now it's the one who came first who counts.

However, a belief in wider opportunities did not necessarily imply a Conservative vote. The other two interviewees who thought that upward mobility had become easier were centrist voters. Ms J, an Alliance voter who last voted Labour in 1966, said: 'I think it has improved. It does seem a bit easier for people to go another step up the ladder. Success seems to be encouraged more, as it is in America. We seem to be getting more like America every day. It probably is due to Mrs Thatcher. She seems to be dashing about and coming back with more ideas, I suppose that's why things are changing.' And Mr N, a floater who voted SDP in 1987, said: 'The chances have improved. It doesn't just rely on paper qualifications. If you've got the inclination then you can get into management and that sort of thing. There's more encouragement for training. Restrictions are disappearing in my company certainly. There's more training.'

On the other hand, a belief that the class divide had become more marked usually ruled out the possibility of voting Tory. Mr A, and an Alliance voter, said: 'I think it's probably harder to get on in life now than it was ten years ago. There are a lot of jobs about but so many of them are badly paid. There are people who have benefited from the Conservatives; they are the self-employed. I've got a friend who has started up his own removal business who never used to bother to vote but he now votes Tory because financially for his company it benefits him. He would be a fool not to.'

Mr B, a non-voter, said: 'I think for working-class people we are going back to the time when it's only the people who have the money to pay for a public school education who have the opportunities. For people like ourselves there is just no way. You go through life hoping to better yourself but at the end of the day it revolves around how much money you can draw in at the end of the week.' 'For the working class it is less easy to get to the top,' said Mr C, an Alliance voter. 'It's only the wealthy that stand a chance of getting anywhere. It's only for the rich, this country, that's why the big companies give so much money to the Tories, they're for the rich. They don't worry about the poor at all.'

Mr S, an SDP redefector to Labour in 1987, said: 'Harder. You get so far and there's a closed gate. But I've always thought that. There hasn't been that much change.' And Ms O, a Liberal, said: 'Not as easy. People are more particular about what jobs they give to individuals. And if you look at judges, there's still not one of them that didn't go to Eton or Cambridge.'

Although the divide between the working class and middle class remains, it is also true, as the previous chapter showed, that a new division has opened up in the 1980s within the working class, between the 'underclass' of the unemployed and low-paid on the one hand and those in secure jobs on the other.

I'm all right, Jack

What about the charge that consumerism makes people less interested in helping those less well off than themselves? Eric Deakins claims: 'Care, concern and compassion became the exception rather than the rule; looking after oneself took precedence over concern for others. People were on their own, dependent increasingly on their own experience and resources. Isolated behind a barrier of possessions and home entertainment, the individual became even more a spectator than a participant in the life of the community' (*What Future for Labour?*, pp. 8–9).

However, the only sense in which the ownership of consumer goods leads to individualism is that they do away with the need for such collectivist experiences as going to the launderette, employing servants and going to the cinema. Sheffield Labour councillor Mukesh Savani tells the story of a council-run launderette in Sheffield which the council decided to close because it was too old and inefficient. The romantic left wing of the local Labour Party immediately began a campaign to 'defend the launderette'. Savani confronted them, saying that for the amount of money the launderette was losing, the council could afford to buy a brand new washing machine for every household which used it. 'But what about the common experience?' came the reply. That the experience of sitting in a line watching the washing go round is an expression of collectivism is of course ridiculous, even if the original provision of the launderette by Sheffield city council in 1926 was an example of collective improvement. But it speaks to a strong sense, very widely felt, of a past collectivist golden age.

It was (or is) a golden age of being in and out of each others' houses. In the discussion group, Janet said:

> I think people are so involved with their selves and their family that they really haven't got much time for anything else, like they used to when I was younger. People used to help people out more. I remember my mum used to have friends, and if they had and she didn't have, then they'd share and they were always in each others' houses, and chatting on doorsteps. I think people have more now, this is what it is. They have more and they're striving to get more, and they haven't got any time for others.

It is certainly true that shorter working hours and longer television-watching hours have had a profound effect on lifestyles. Attitudes towards time itself have probably changed, but there is no reason why this has to mean that people are more selfish, materialistic or individualistic. But the style of collectivism has changed, that instead of solidarity of mass labour forces we now have the mass media solidarity of Live Aid.

Summary

This chapter set out to answer two questions. Do rising living standards (a) make people more likely to vote Conservative, and (b) make people more individualistic in their values? To which the answers are: Yes, in the short term, and No.

There has been a panic in some of the more romantic or nostalgic parts of the Labour Party, both left and right, that the spread of fridges, videos and other home comforts is weakening the bonds of working-class solidarity – a panic that more or less exactly mirrors that of 1959–62, when material benefits of the 'you've never had it so good' era were thought to have had a corrosive effect on the Labour Party's support. Harold Wilson's election as prime minister in 1964 demonstrated the fallacy of that fear, and, although Labour on its own now has much further to go to recover power in 1991, the Conservative government was also less popular in 1987 than it was in 1959, winning only 42 per cent of the vote instead of 49 per cent.

The theory that the working class was becoming more 'middle class' in its political values in the late 1950s and early 1960s was also disproved by academic studies. Although the working class has shrunk and the middle class expanded, there is no evidence that the values of the working class are changing in the late 1970s and 1980s either. The Conservative policy which most directly attempts to relate individual prosperity with support for individualist political values, that of holding down public spending on health, education and welfare services in order to deliver income tax cuts, has failed to win support for those values. When Margaret Thatcher came to power, opinion was equally divided as to the desirability of tax cuts versus better services; now there is approximately a seven-to-one majority for better services.

Political values have not changed because underlying class realities have not changed. Although the country as a whole is richer than it was in 1979, this prosperity has been geographically and socially skewed by the unbalanced recovery of the economy since 1982. The income gap between middle-class and working-class jobs has widened sharply: in 1979 non-manual earnings were on average 21 per cent higher than manual earnings, in 1986 the differential had widened to 40 per cent.[8] And the very gradual trend towards a more equal relative distribution of wealth has been halted, while absolute differences in wealth have increased sharply. What is more, despite the expansion of further education and middle-class employment, the difference between the life-chances of working-class people and those of middle-class people are unchanged.

If Mrs Thatcher had been successful in fooling most of the people that now 'we are all working people', these objective realities would not matter. But she hasn't. The way people see British society hasn't changed: 'You get so far and there's a closed gate.' Some of our interviewees think that getting to the top in Britain is easier than it was, but others think it is harder.

What the Conservatives have done very successfully is to incorporate the idea of 'bettering oneself' into the Tory identity. This enables them to take full advantage of the usual tendency for people whose living standards are rising to support the party in power. But this cannot go on for ever. The Conservatives have managed to sustain weak economic growth for long enough, and concentrated enough on a sufficiently large section of the population, to win two elections. Either most people will go on getting richer until they want not just a better car or a better house, but to live in a better society; or growth will falter, in which case 'leave it to the market' will not be a credible economic policy.

10
Morality

Some people are kind and caring within their own family,
[but] you can be self-centred towards your own family and
forget about society as a whole. I think everybody, not only
for good and bad reasons, needs other people.

Margaret Thatcher's famous declaration that 'there is no such thing
as society' was offered in the middle of her explanation as to why
there had been a deterioration in the nation's moral standards, a
question put to her by *Woman's Own* (31 October 1987).

I think we've been through a period where too many people
have been given to understand that if they have problem it's the
government's job to cope with it. 'I have a problem, I'll get a
grant.' 'I'm homeless, the government must house me.' They're
casting their problem on society. And, you know, there is no such
thing as society. There are individual men and women, and there
are families. And no government can do anything except through
people, and people must look to themselves first. It's our duty to
look after ourselves and then, also, to look after our neighbour.

This anti-social morality (anti-social in the sense of being anti-
society) is central to Mrs Thatcher's attempted revolution. Winning
the hearts and minds of the people to this fundamental moral
value is the key to her claimed success in establishing individual
responsibility as the basis of support for political individualism.

Note how unconvincingly Mrs Thatcher tacked on 'our neighbour' to the end of her sentence. Neighbourliness could be the
beginnings of 'society', and so she makes sure that it stops before
it extends as far as next-door-but-one. She continued: 'People have
got the entitlements too much in mind, without the obligations.
There's no such thing as entitlement, unless someone has first

139

met an obligation.' Instead of 'society', there is only a network of reciprocal contracts between autonomous individuals. But looking after our neighbour is a moral injunction which should be obeyed regardless of whether that neighbour has first met an obligation – a neighbour is entitled to be looked after simply by virtue of being nearby. This is the germ of the idea of citizenship – that people have entitlements simply by virtue of being members of a society – and it is the hole in the middle of Mrs Thatcher's doughnut morality.

The morality of individualism is one-sided, emphasising responsibility and self-discipline at the expense of compassion and selflessness. Ever since the war (and before), people have bemoaned the lack of a national spirit, a willingness to make sacrifices for the general good. The 'I'm Backing Britain' campaign in the 1960s was a strong grassroots expression of this feeling. But the Thatcher governments have, literally, made a virtue out of this lack of collective solidarity (or, at least, the seizing up of mechanisms by which it might be expressed). They have undermined what remaining foundations such solidarity might have, and proclaimed a morality which begins and ends, like charity, at home.

Fortunately, the government has been entirely unsuccessful in its moral putsch – because, in the end, it doesn't satisfy people's desire for a renewed community spirit. There is a postscript to the 'I'm Backing Britain' story which illustrates this well. Carol Monahan was one of the women who started the campaign in 1968 when she was a 16-year-old typist at Colt Ventilation. Looking back twenty years later, she said: 'I suppose you could say that all we really achieved by getting people to work an extra half hour every day was to make their employers richer.' But she defends the patriotic motive behind it and criticises the selfishness, greed and materialism of the 1980s.

If you want to achieve something Britain is a good place to live. But if you can't look after yourself, it isn't such a good place any more. In 1968, it never really occurred to me to question the way society works. Today, I have a job with the Social Services, working with elderly people. And I have a son who suffers from a rare genetic disorder. As a result I look at Britain much more from the point of view of the less fortunate members of society.

Paradoxically, she was being interviewed for the *Sunday Telegraph*'s colour supplement (3 January 1988); for its 'My Country

Right or Wrong?' feature, which so successfully taps the feeling of moral decline, the deep reservoir of 'Things ain't what they used to be' which often passes for patriotism in Britain today.

If the decline of community spirit was evident to Carol Monahan and her friends in 1968, Norman Tebbit dates the beginning of the decline in moral standards from precisely that date. According to him, it was 1960s permissiveness that was the cause of most modern ills. And, while Ms Monahan feels that things have gone from bad to worse in the 1980s, dedicated Conservatives pretend to recognise a moral revival since 1979 – although they do keep forgetting the party line in their haste to denounce the spread of wickedness, criminality and the dependency culture.

That the moral decline had continued through the 1980s was beyond doubt, according to the two groups of former Labour voters in their discussions. 'You've only got to pick up a paper, and you hear of old people being mugged, more rapes,' said Jack. 'I think values have changed a great deal, there's no respect for people any more.' Tony said: 'Yes, I agree with that. I mean, when we was kids we used to go out and play and that. But now you can't let them out because someone might come and nick them.' Jonathan added: 'There's no respect for the old.'

In order to find out more about this common feeling of moral decline, the groups were asked why they thought fewer people go to church nowadays, and whether this meant moral values had changed. Lynn's explanation was that 'there's more to do now, there's television and all that. If you've got the choice of going ice-skating or going to sit in a church, I know what I'd do. I think people are a lot more materialistic now.' According to Jonathan, 'it's very boring in church'.

None of either group went to church regularly – 'just christenings, weddings and Christmas' – and the pressure of time was frequently cited as an explanation both of this and of declining moral standards. 'Time is at a premium now,' said David.

Jane observed: 'If you go into a church, it seems to miss the middle generation out. You either get the mums with the younger children, or the younger children with the teenagers, and then older people, but it seems to miss out the middle years. People are so busy with their lives.'

Pressure of time also explained the spread of general rudeness, according to Janet: 'Everyone's in such a rush. Everyone's just rushing around and getting this and getting that.' Selfishness seems new because it is associated with what makes life modern: the city, where time goes faster and buying things fills the spiritual vacuum.

Sylvia said: 'Churchgoing is very much a community spirit. Perhaps in small places people still gather round and see each other. I think London hasn't got much community spirit around, I think people are terribly individual.'

Lynn agreed: 'Villages go.' She blamed acquisitiveness. 'Fifty years ago, children weren't all out smashing shops, because there wasn't any point in being nasty, robbing banks, because it just wasn't around. But now people want more, everybody wants more.'

Jane blamed this in turn on the mass media: 'What worries me is we judge ourselves on what the media say to us is supposed to be the norm. So whatever they're projecting and saying we should have, because we haven't got all the materialistic things we feel that we're not good enough.'

Di asserted the connection between self-reliance and selfishness which Mrs Thatcher explicitly denies; because she had to work, she wasn't always at home when her children came home from school, so 'they had to look after themselves a little bit and maybe that makes them a bit more selfish'. Being made to stand on their own two feet turned them into anti-social monsters, not model citizens.

Janet had a simpler explanation: 'They get too much. When I was young, best clothes were worn only on Sunday, and I got new clothes Easter, birthdays and Christmas. Whereas my little one, you know, if she wants a pair of shoes she'll have a pair of shoes and if she wants a new jacket that's in, she'll have a new jacket that's in. And I can't say no, because it's the way things are now. Her life would just be made such hell at school because she's out of date or scruffy or a fleabag. It's dreadful.'

Di added: 'And presents too. I remember that we got bicycles for Christmas, I think I was 13 and had that bicycle till I was 18 and it was secondhand when it was new. Nowadays kids get a bike at nine or ten and then they get another one every two years, you know, like you change your car.'

The decline of morals is a curious historical phenomenon. The women in the discussion group seemed to resent their children for their 'better life', which they had just agreed doesn't exist any more.

The men's golden age was more to do with the world of work. 'When I think back to when I started work, there was so much full employment then. Everybody seemed to be aiming for a thing in life. They worked hard, they got things out of their own lives, they built their families up and so forth,' said Jonathan. 'But nowadays there doesn't seem to be any end product to people. They seem to want aggravation, to get everything quickly, because they don't know what's going to happen in the next ten, fifteen years.'

Brian added: 'It's generating a system of people becoming more selfish.' Sixty-one per cent of the population agree with him; only 19 per cent think the British have become more generous in the past ten years (Harris poll for *The Observer*, 22 May 1988). Looking after number one is clearly not thought to be the path to true happiness either: only 21 per cent thought that people were happier.

Pulpit politics

Mrs Thatcher was aware that her individualism was in danger of being seen as an endorsement of this unhappy selfishness. Hence her 'Sermon on the Mound', her address to the General Assembly of the Church of Scotland in May 1988, an attempt to defend her anti-society morality – an attempt that only succeeded in making matters worse. Not only was she prepared to defend selfishness (so it seemed), but she was also prepared to quote selectively from the Bible to do so. Her interpretation of the Bible as justifying the desire for wealth was stunningly implausible: 'Abundance rather than poverty has a legitimacy which derives from the very nature of Creation,' she said. But she had reluctantly to admit: 'Nevertheless, the Tenth Commandment – Thou shalt not covet – recognises that making money and owning things could become selfish activities. But it is not the creation of wealth that is wrong, but love of money for its own sake.'

She has always advertised the morality of money-making, for example demanding rhetorically: 'Isn't it moral that people should want to improve the standard of living for their family by their own efforts? Isn't it moral that families should work for the means to look after their own folk? Isn't it moral that people should save in order to be responsible for themselves in later life?' (5 June 1987).

And she had been given to bizarre interpretations of biblical lessons before, such as: 'No one would have remembered the

Good Samaritan if he'd only had good intentions – he had money as well' (*Weekend World*, 6 January 1980). But her Edinburgh address was unique in its scope and ambition. And, by drawing attention to the shaky theological foundation of her 'absolute moral values', it also drew attention to how far outside the central British tradition of moral values she actually is. That tradition is shaped by Christianity, but a Christianity which is only dimly recognisable from Mrs Thatcher's account of it. Her emphasis on the '*Judaic*-Christian tradition' is an attempt to get away from the New Testament, the original collectivist and anti-materialist manifesto, which is much more important than the ('Judaic') Old Testament to the various Protestantisms which form the dominant British religious tradition.

Mrs Thatcher quoted ten words from St Paul ('if a man will not work he shall not eat') which are a travesty of the main thrust of Pauline philosophy. Bishop John Robinson, who was an authority on this subject, had pre-empted her thirty-six years ago: 'Christians should be the last people to be found clinging to the wrecks of an atomistic individualism, which has no foundation in the Bible . . . Paul starts, as we do, from the fact that man is bound up in a vast solidarity of historical existence which denies him the freedom to control his own destiny. The great corporations of modern society are expressions of this all-embracing solidarity. The temptation of western man is to seek salvation by exalting the individual *against* such collectives. Paul saw that the Christian gospel is very different . . . Solidarity is the divinely ordained structure in which personal life is to be lived.'[1]

For Mrs Thatcher, the idea that collective organisations or collective material provision can express a sense of all-embracing solidarity is incomprehensible. She believes that the pursuit of economic equality is divisive. And her Home Secretary, Douglas Hurd, says that equality actually corrodes morality. This is a third Tory explanation for the moral decline over which they have presided. Mrs Thatcher blames it on the illusion that there is such a thing as society, Mr Tebbit blames it on flower power and free love; Douglas Hurd blames it on excessive equality: 'Social cohesion is quite different from social equality; indeed the two are ultimately incompatible.'[2]

Mrs Thatcher believes that the 'spirit and solidarity of the nation' can only be expressed and renewed through nationalism, or by everyone sharing the same moral values – as long as they are 'traditional' ones. Difficulties arise for Conservatives when one of the moral values which does actually unite the nation is that of the desirability of greater material equality. Hence the Tory emphasis on *traditional* moral values, which are really rules of social conformity rather than ethical imperatives.

Traditional moral values are therefore an important part of Tory individualism, because they propose no change to the existing social order. True morality, on the other hand, requires society as a whole to accept its responsibilities for the life of all its members. Indeed, to the extent that traditional moral values involve respect for authority, they reinforce the existing social order. Chapter 8 also showed how disciplinarian attitudes towards social security scroungers can undermine support for collective provision for the unemployed.

Moral traditionalism on specific social issues such as sex equality, homosexuality, race and hanging, can be measured over the late 1970s and 1980s – the period in which profound shifts in the electorate's values are supposed to have occurred. For the future, the British Social Attitudes series will also provide a wealth of information about authoritarianism in general, with its questions about whether 'schools should teach children to obey authority' (83 per cent agree) and 'even wrong laws should be obeyed' (46 per cent agree).

Popular attitudes on the social issues which make up the traditionalists' battleground are not as authoritarian as they are sometimes caricatured. The instinct of toleration is stronger than opinion poll findings suggest, and the support for capital punishment is hedged about with an awareness of the practical drawbacks. Furthermore, the tide is not flowing against liberalism, with the exception of attitudes to homosexuality. After the rapid progress in legislation and public opinion in the 1960s, the forward march of liberal social values is hesitating. Racial prejudice remains an unmoving, ugly obstacle to social progress, but public opinion is still moving in a liberal direction on sex equality and hanging. And getting back to the intolerant position of the 1940s and 1950s on any of these issues is quite beyond the reach of the traditionalists.

Paul Johnson was premature in claiming, in the *Daily Mail* (19 October 1987), that 'the Thatcher spirit, having conquered politically, having turned round the country economically, is now beginning to have an impact at the fundamental levels of our national culture – on the way all of us think and behave.' He alleged that 'there are signs that the permissive era in Britain is coming to an end and that the country is moving slowly but surely back to traditional values'. What were these signs? He cited the pressure to restrict abortion and the dislike of 'public posturings' of gays. 'Above all,' he says, 'capital punishment may once more become an open issue.' That is a big change. 'On this point, the majority of the British public has never accepted the permissive creed.' So what was this fundamental change in the way we think and behave? All the same, he concludes: 'Moral relativism is on its way out and the reign of the Ten Commandments is returning.' (You know, the Ten Commandments that begin: Thou shalt not be homosexual; Thou shalt not have an abortion; Thou shalt not kill, except people who disobey this Commandment . . .)

Turning from the wishful delusions of a converted zealot to the evidence, the proportion of the population thinking 'attempts to ensure equality for women have gone too far' has halved since the 1970s, while that thinking they have not gone far enough reached 42 per cent in 1987.[3]

	Too far %	Not far enough %
1974	19	35
1978	20	17
1979	23	29
1981	12	31
1983	9	32
1987	11	42

Some of the fall in reactionary views is probably explained by the fact that the 1974–9 Labour government did actually make some attempts to ensure equality for women, while Mrs Thatcher's governments have not been conspicuous in their endeavours. But the progressive trend is unmistakable.

More liberal attitudes to divorce are also discernible. Support for each of ten possible grounds for divorce rose by between 1 and 15 percentage points between 1981 and 1986.[4] 'Traditional' moral attitudes to marriage are overwhelmingly unpopular – only 23 per

146

cent believe that sex before marriage is 'always' or 'mostly' wrong (while fidelity is a universal value, with 82 per cent believing that sex *outside* marriage is always or mostly wrong).[5]

There is also evidence of a trend towards more liberal views on abortion, despite the unsuccessful attempts to restrict women's right to choose with the Corrie Bill in 1980 and the Alton Bill in 1988. The percentages thinking 'the availability of abortion on the NHS has gone too far' were:[6]

	%
1974	43
1978	33
1979	44
1981	29
1983	32
1987	30

The trend towards support for sex equality has been evident since the start of opinion polling in Britain in 1937. In 1938 Gallup asked 'Do you think a woman should be barred from any form of employment simply because she is married?' and 28 per cent said 'Yes' (63 per cent said 'No'). But between 1947 and 1969 Gallup found a steady decline in the proportion who disapproved of 'women being paid the same wages as men if they are doing the same work' from 36 to 19 per cent.

Attitudes towards homosexuals show the most clear-cut illiberal trend, as a result of the prominence given to homosexuality by publicity about Aids and by the tabloid newspaper campaign against gay rights. Gallup found a rise from 63 to 75 per cent in the proportion saying that 'homosexuals should not be allowed to adopt children' between 1979 and 1986, and a rise from 23 to 33 per cent in those who thought 'homosexual relations between consenting adults should not be legal'. However, in the permissive 1960s even more people were opposed to the legalisation of private homosexual behaviour between men over 21 (39 per cent in 1966, the year before it was actually decriminalised). The British Social Attitudes survey also found an increase between 1983 and 1985 in those thinking homosexual relationships were always or mostly wrong, from 62 to 69 per cent.[7]

The discussion groups showed that attitudes are much more mixed than these figures seem to suggest. Homosexuality was generally thought to be 'unnatural', but nobody's business as long as it was not 'forced down people's throats' and especially as long as children were kept in strict ignorance of it. The first sentiment in the women's discussion, launched by Lynn, who was fairly 'Thatcherite' on most things, was a tolerant one: 'Whatever people want, as long as it doesn't bother me in particular.' Ann said: 'It makes me feel sick. When you see it on the TV, you know, these men kissing, I think that's disgusting. There's no need to show it.' Di said: 'I think it can be pushed down your throat a little bit, which I don't really like very much. [But] it doesn't necessarily make them bad people.'

Wendy said: 'We've got a few friends, both male and female, who are gay and I don't mind them at all, but I wouldn't want my children to grow up to be gay. It's still an unnatural thing, to me. I don't like the idea of kids at school having these books to read to make out that it's all quite normal because to me I don't think that it is.'

Di was the only one to bring in the question of unfair discrimination: 'I think it's a good thing that it's more acceptable in that [society] doesn't discriminate against people because they're one way or the other, because I don't think that in their ordinary everyday life people should be discriminated against. But they're talking about homosexuality in the church and whether people would accept if their minister is gay. Well, I would find it pretty hard to accept, especially if he was taking my children for communion classes. I would feel uneasy about it. But it doesn't morally make them bad.'

The men combined toleration and disgust in similar measures. 'I don't reckon it ought to be publicised as much as it is – to bring it out as though it's natural and normal for people to be like that. Especially when they start trying to teach it to them in schools, in books and things, that is definitely out of order,' said Jack.

'I don't think it should be rammed down people's throats, but other than that it should be acceptable. I mean I've worked with two or three and they seemed quite nice,' said David, to raucous laughter. 'You know what I mean, not as bad as the stories that people tend to put around, like you put your backside against the wall as you walk along, but as ordinary people they seemed to be okay.'

Jonathan said: 'I think it must corrupt young people. No doubt about it, young people are always corruptible at a young age. And the more you push it on them, the more they think, "oh this is good, we're going to try that", even though they may not be that way inclined, they'll do it and they'll get into a hell of a . . . you know, other things.'

Whether attitudes to racial discrimination have changed in the 1980s is not clear. Gallup recorded 4-point rises in the percentages of people regarding 'immigrants, foreign workers' or 'people of a different race' as 'groups of people that you would not like to have as neighbours' between 1982 and 1986.[8] On the question of whether 'attempts to ensure equality for coloured people have gone too far' there is no decisive trend (the question wording was changed to 'black people and Asians' in 1983).

	Too far %	Not far enough %
1974	27	29
1978	30	21
1979	30	29
1981	25	31
1983	20	27

There was no significant change in the number of people describing themselves as prejudiced against people of other races between 1983 and 1986, according to the British Social Attitudes surveys: 35 and 36 per cent. But the same two surveys found a significant *decrease* in those who 'would mind if one of their close relatives were to marry an Asian or black person', from 54 to 48 per cent.[9]

In the group discussions there was a strong sense that attempts to secure racial equality had gone too far, although the 'send 'em back' instinct was challenged by the more liberal members of both groups. The focus of this sense of grievance was elusive when probed. It was a resentment *against* a consensus, the anti-racist consensus which prevented people 'saying what they think'.

Carol said: 'I think they should most of them go back. Especially the ones that come over here and can't speak any English. I think it's wrong. They should lead an English way of life.'

'But don't forget,' said Di, 'when you're talking about racial discrimination you're talking about not just black people, you're talking about people from every country in the world.'

This didn't mean anything to the rest of the group. Ann went on to say: 'I don't think the Asians are too bad actually, the ones I've mixed with and that, shopkeepers. Where we live it's just the Asians have got the shops and they're very polite and nice. The blacks worry me more.'

Janet said: 'I think the older ones are fine and they're even ashamed of their own younger ones, how they perform. They are very aggressive. I suppose in the past they have had good reason,' she admitted. 'But that was so long ago, and they are getting it so good now. I mean they *are* equal, it's all geared to minorities. It seems to me that we are being pushed further and further away. It seems they are allowed to get away with much more, because they shout discrimination, all the time.' Asked if she could give an example, there was a long pause. 'Papers are not allowed to say it was two black guys that beat up this woman. They can say it was two white men, they can say things like that. The media are not allowed to say it was a black person, or that black people are doing more of this now. Nobody is allowed to say what they feel. You're just frightened. If you have a row with some black person, then it's racial discrimination. I don't know, it's all madness. And I think we're being pushed further and further away.' This sense of exclusion among white people is frequently identified by them with anti-racist policies, and it is one of the failures of anti-racism in Britain that it hasn't devised strategies for overcoming it.

David echoed her complaint that equality had gone too far: 'I think personally it's gone the other way. As white people we're scared to say anything about the black race generally. You really have to watch what you're saying, particularly at work. I think it's just gone completely nuts.'

'Enoch Powell hit it on the head years ago when he said ship them all back home, don't even allow any more in,' said Jack, and Tony agreed: 'He was right. Definitely right.' Of the men, only Brian held out: 'I suppose we all know a couple of people here and there who are good friends. I think the trouble is, it only takes a few of them to abuse the system. And perhaps we tend to leap on the band-wagon and tar them all with the same brush. If that's the right expression.'

The trend of public opinion on capital punishment is confused by changes in question wording. In the 1960s support for the abolition of hanging varied between 18 and 22 per cent (British Election Studies) and up to 25 per cent (Gallup).[10] The death penalty was abolished temporarily in 1965 and permanently in 1969. The British Election Studies showed a sharp increase in the percentage favouring its abolition from 25 to 37 per cent between 1979 and 1983; this huge jump isn't repeated in Gallup's polls, although the direction of change in its differently worded question was the same. Those opposing the death penalty increased from an average of 17 per cent in 1979 to 23 per cent in 1987.[11] British Social Attitudes surveys show no significant change between 1983 and 1985.[12] The attitudes of the discussion groups to the issue helps explain why opinion poll answers are so sensitive to differently worded questions: for many people their first authoritarian instinct could be modified quickly when different implications of the issue were mentioned by others in the group.

Among the women the immediate instinct for blood was softened and then pushed back first by Di, a liberal Conservative, and then, more surprisingly, by Janet, a keen Thatcherite. Wendy (a reluctant SDP voter) was most hard line: 'For child murderers, definitely. [Pause.] Not so much crimes of passion, but definitely people that have killed children.'

But Di said: 'I don't think that I could sit in a jury and say: "Yes, that man should hang." ' And Janet asked: 'What would you think if it was your own son or daughter that was going to be hung? It's all very well for you to say that, but if it was your own son or daughter that was for the hanging, and if they were innocent? There's always that.' To which Wendy replied: 'Well, hopefully that would never arise.'

Both Carol and Jane typified the instinct for vengeance tempered by doubts. Carol said: 'I'm not sure really, because I'd like them to suffer. But then they might be innocent.' And Jane said: 'I don't know. I'm quite undecided about it, really. I think your initial reaction is – isn't it? – to say "yes", but then when you think about it . . . Certainly sentences should be longer.'

Among the men, there was more unanimity, although opinion surveys show no significant difference in attitudes between the sexes.[13] Tony said: 'Bring it back. It's got to happen sooner or later, because it's getting out of order.' He and Jack were keen to see hanging restored for all sorts of things, but the others wanted it used sparingly. David said: 'Bring it back for certain cases, not as a

matter of course. Killing policemen, perhaps, and prison warders.'
Hugh would agree to it only for child murders. But even Brian, the
lone non-Tory, conceded: 'Yes, for certain things.'

Social authoritarianism is not as strong as it sometimes seems
when looking at unadorned opinion poll figures; nor is it getting
stronger, apart from the setback in the long-term trend towards
greater toleration of homosexuality. There have been no dramatic
shifts in popular values under Mrs Thatcher, but there is a better
case for saying that the electorate is moving from authoritarianism
to liberalism in its social values than from collectivism to individualism in its economic values.

Charity begins at home

When it comes to economic morality, the discussion groups were
roughly divided between Mrs Thatcher's anti-society morality and a
collectivist ethic. They were asked about charity in order to discover
how far their concept of society extended.

For Lynn charity was a matter of being able to identify with
those less fortunate than yourself: 'A lot of them you can relate
to, disasters like the Zeebrugge. I mean probably most people
have been on it. And children starving. You would relate to it if
you've got children of your own.' But the willingness to identify
with people in the Third World is limited. 'A lot of people think
that charity begins at home. [And] if it's a case of us starving
or them starving, well then obviously you do think that, don't
you? I mean you've got to put yourself and your own family
first.'

Di said: 'When you see pictures of Ethiopia it tears your heart
out. I know it's only just there now and it soon fades away, but
really that's why I do the NSPCC. If there's so much given to
worldwide charities, the ones I want to support are the ones that
are here, in this country, who are working hard.'

Jack, despite being a strong Conservative, explained why there
was a greater need for individual charity: 'The government used
to look after people more than what they do now.' Brian (an SDP
voter) agreed: 'Yes, I think they don't look after people very well,
this present government. Strong Tory governments have always
been the same as far as I can see. They're a very hard party,

aren't they? They just want to get the economy straight. I think that's bad. They make a few token gestures as far as people are concerned. The economy will still be around in a hundred years.'

The fact that Mrs Thatcher's individualist morality is out of touch with the moral traditions of real people was well illustrated when the groups were asked what makes someone a good person. 'A kind person. Someone that thinks about other people, not someone that's totally self-centred,' said Wendy.

'But some people are kind and caring within their own family and they think that's really good, and other people would think they were quite selfish because they weren't kind and caring to society as a whole,' said Jane, to which Wendy responded: 'I meant to society as a whole.'

Jane continued: 'You can be self-centred towards your own family and forget about . . . I think everybody, not only for good and bad reasons, needs other people. I would always be hopeful that I could keep my friends and perhaps be kind to somebody that needs a bit of help or something. Not all the time, because it wouldn't be possible, but maybe in a small way. It's hard to spread yourself about too much when you've got a family to bring up.'

The women were also unanimous when they were asked whether they wanted to protect the NHS for the sake of society as a whole, or simply for themselves and their families. Di said: 'For society, because I hate to see these awful stories about people waiting two and three years, children dying for lack of nurses to care for them, wards being closed and new hospitals being built and we just don't have the nurses for them.'

Obviously, it is easier to find support for a collective morality on the collectivist home ground of the NHS. But it does indicate the political potential of collective morality among non-Labour voters. And only Jack ('people should be self-sufficient') and David adopted the classic Thatcherite creed: 'People should be self-reliant. I think people should tend to look after themselves, and perhaps a very close-knit group, within the family.'

This was not a popular position. Brian said: 'I don't agree with that. I think it would be rather nice if we had a society where we could look after people who are less able to afford things than ourselves.'

153

Summary

Mrs Thatcher has tried for nearly ten years to change the moral values of the nation. Her individualist morality is the foundation stone of her political revolution. But while a political revolution of sorts has been taking place, the foundations of political morality remain firmly established elsewhere, waiting for what Kenneth Baker called the architecture of collectivism to be rebuilt on them.

Mrs Thatcher's political morality is anti-social in that it regards society as a 'fictious body' and hence not a proper object of moral sentiment. The moral traditions of the generality of the British people, on the other hand, while they may not be unambiguously collectivist or socialist, are certainly social. One of the teacherly examples Mrs Thatcher used to make her point about there being 'no such thing as society' is telling. 'I'm homeless, the government must house me,' she said, mimicking the feckless whine of an imaginary dependent of the dependency culture. Yet the people overwhelmingly support the view that it is the government's responsibility to ensure that everyone has a decent place to live.

This gap between government and people sufficiently alarmed the Prime Minister that it drove her to religion in her speech to the Church of Scotland, in May 1988. The next day *The Observer* published its finding that three-fifths of the population thought that Britain had become a more selfish country under her government. But it is precisely because the electorate doesn't believe in the Thatcherite religion of self-interest that she has to lecture them on how compatible it is with their old one. Seventy per cent of the population may believe in God, but he or she is mostly a New Testament God of selflessness and a bias to the poor.[14]

So Conservatives try to restrict the concept of morality to so-called traditional moral values. This is safer territory for them, because the British are economically radical but socially conservative. But it is territory that is shrinking, despite the 1980s backlash against homosexuals. Social authoritarianism, which is useful to Conservatives in undermining economic radicalism (for example in attitudes to social security scroungers), is in long-term decline. And the attitudes of the discussion groups towards social issues were more complicated and tolerant than might have been expected from their initial responses to questions, suggesting that opinion surveys on subjects like homosexuality and hanging may overestimate authoritarian attitudes.

The bastion of traditional values, the family, remains at the centre of most people's moral universe, but they don't want it to be the isolated unit of Mrs Thatcher's atomised society. Our interviews and group discussions showed a strong desire for caring to go beyond the immediate family and for greater social solidarity outside the household. While Mrs Thatcher wants to go no further than the neighbour, and only that far if the neighbour has been good and carried out his or her reciprocal duties.

11

A Collective Future

Individualism and collectivism are cumbersome words with which to analyse British politics, and especially the political views of the majority of people who don't think of themselves as being interested in politics. However, they have advantages over the terms left, right and centre, which are too broad and flexible to be of much use. The word socialism, too, bears the weight of too much history, and is too identified with the Labour Party, which is only one part (albeit the larger part) of the opposition to Tory individualism. Other possible labels, such as radical, reactionary and conservative are even less useful, because they depend on what it is that is being radically changed, reacted against or conserved. Individualism and collectivism indicate, quite precisely, the different views of society which most divide Thatcherites and non-Thatcherites.

Of course, the political values of ordinary people do not fall into such a simple pattern. Individualism and collectivism are often not seen as opposites; and other, quite different, values and issues also affect the way people vote. But they go to the heart of how party loyalties are formed. 'Partisanship appears to be organised around two ideological dimensions,' according to John Curtice in his analysis of the kind of questions which most divide supporters of the three main parties.

> One centres on the value of collective action to achieve equality and divides Conservatives from Labour, with the Alliance either equidistant or somewhat to the right. The second encompasses both traditional liberal values concerning the relationship between the individual and the state, and a social democratic concern with the role of the welfare state; this dimension divides Conservatives from both Labour and the Alliance. (*British Social Attitudes: The 1986 Report*, p. 50)

156

There is a tension between the collectivism of working-class solidarity in the first dimension and the collectivism of the welfare state
in the second, which means that there are important differences
between the political values of Labour and Democrat supporters:
the social bases of the two parties are different. Labour's political
values are still shaped largely by class while the Democrats' values
are shaped more by education, because the core of the third-party
vote consists of middle-class graduates. But the distinctive values of
centre-party voters are shared with Labour voters: they are support
for the welfare state and for civil liberties.

The centre parties have been just as critical as Labour of the
selfishness and acquisitiveness of modern Toryism. And the political
philosophy of Paddy Ashdown (such as it is) and David Marquand
(guru to the social democratic wing of the SLD) is indistinguishable
from that of the Labour Party's 1988 *Statement of Aims and Values*.
So it is perfectly legitimate to regard the 57 per cent vote against
Mrs Thatcher in 1987 as a collectivist majority, and as much more
of a coherent political force than the anti-socialist majority of 68
per cent who voted against the Labour Party.

But whether collectivist values will actually be put into practice
in the 1990s depends on the party political battle for the leadership
of the non-Conservative forces. In order to predict the outcome of
the battle between Labour and the Democrats, let alone to assist
it, the nature of Labour's failure and the centre's success need to
be understood.

The Labour Party has been a singularly unsuccessful organisation
in the past ten years. That is as obvious as these things can be to
everyone apart from Tony Benn, who asserted that Labour's 28
per cent vote in the 1983 General Election was a high point in the
progress towards utopia, because it represented 'eight-and-a-half
million votes for socialism'. What is less obvious, however, is that
the Conservatives have been just as unsuccessful. This may seem to
be as startlingly silly as Benn's 1983 analysis, but it can be backed
up by evidence.

The shift from blue-collar to white-collar employment is eroding
the Labour Party's base and assisting the Conservatives and the
centre parties. But, if social changes are taken into account, then
both Labour and the Conservatives have performed less well, and
the Liberals and the Alliance better, than would be expected.[1]
Looked at in the context of electoral trends over a quarter-century,

the *political* failure of the Conservatives in the 1987 General Election was just as dramatic as that of the Labour Party. But the Conservatives' failure was disguised by the growth of middle-class occupations (and, marginally, by the spread of home ownership), whereas Labour's failure was exaggerated by the shrinking of the manual working class (and, marginally, by the contraction of trade union membership).

It is not yet fashionable to say so, but the surprising fact of recent political history is the extent of Margaret Thatcher's ideological failure. With all the advantages of holding power, economic growth and social change in her favour, she has failed to increase the Conservative percentage of the vote at two successive General Elections. And she has failed to shift the electorate from its collectivist values.

Much of the analysis of 'Thatcherism' has been misdirected. The explanation of Mrs Thatcher's political dominance has not been that she has won the arguments – free-market think-tankies may have roamed freely over the government machine under her control, but her three terms in office have simply not been accompanied by a revolution in popular attitudes. Her 'regime' (her own word) is much less securely based than that.[2] The explanation of her dominance is the 'politics of division': the divided opposition in a two-party voting system and the steady but unequal economic growth achieved since 1982.

If Mrs Thatcher hadn't concentrated the benefits of economic growth on her own supporters and potential supporters, and made sure that it was those who didn't vote for her anyway who bore the brunt of her fiscal resolution, then the Conservatives' ideological failure would have been more apparent. The growth rate achieved since 1982 has been low by historical standards, but was skewed towards the South-East and in favour of people already in secure jobs.

The fact that the Conservative and Labour parties have both failed to hold onto their historical levels of support in their social heartlands draws attention to the relative success of the centre parties. In the 1980s the centre parties did well out of the fact that both Labour and the Tories were widely seen as having become more extreme. The Tories failed to hold onto their natural class base because of their unpopular policies embodying unpopular values of selfishness and greed. But how did the Labour

Party lose out to centre parties representing similar, more popular values?

It is difficult for Labour Party supporters to admit that the Social Democrats' breakaway in 1981 was actually *about* anything, but defence policy, the role of trade unions and Labour's record and image in local government all clearly helped the centre parties at Labour's expense. The Labour Party also inherited from the Callaghan government the reputation for incompetence in economic management and an inability to control public employees – a reputation in both particulars not improved by the image of a few Labour councils.

However, the 1987 election demonstrated that these factors taken together were no longer shifting support from Labour to the Alliance. British politics seemed to be more or less frozen in a 40-30-20 formation. Nothing is fixed in politics, and much of this book demonstrates that the *potential* for Labour support is greater than is often thought. But the ability of either opposition party to change its image or leadership is limited.

A popular front

The alternative to waiting for other parties to screw something up or for other external unforeseen events to come to their aid is for Labour and the Democrats to cooperate against the Conservatives. But the way political parties and the electoral system work produces strong, mutually repellent forces. Activists in both parties would find it offensive, especially if it got to the stage where candidates were required to stand down in elections. Labour would suffer from appearing defeatist, while the Democrats would lose a substantial segment of their electoral support because, while more Democrats are closer to Labour, many centre-party supporters would be more horrified at the idea of assisting the Labour Party than at the prospect of helping the Tories. Opinion polls show that supporters of the centre party are twice as likely strongly to dislike the Conservatives as Labour, but 13 per cent of them are still strongly or very strongly against the Labour Party.[3]

But other repellent forces are being removed, or are removing themselves. David Owen's political self-destruction has been useful to the cause of an anti-Conservative popular front, as he always made it abundantly clear that he viewed the prospect of dealing with the Labour Party in a hung parliament with distaste, and the feeling was mutual. And the other three of the original Gang of Four who 'betrayed' the Labour Party by forming the SDP have all removed themselves from active electoral politics.

Meanwhile, there has been a modest but significant shift in local government. On hung councils, where no party has an overall majority, until recently the tendency had been for the Alliance parties to do deals with Conservatives (as much because of fundamentalist Labour hostility as because of any political affinity the Alliance had with the Tories); since 1986 the Alliance, and now the Democrats, have tended to side with Labour.[4]

But a formal pact at national level is fairly unlikely to be signed before the next election. More possible is that the two parties should be increasingly open towards each other and that they should develop formally or informally a common front on values and policies. The purpose of such loose cooperation would be to tie the Democrats by implication and expectation to common policies with Labour in a hung parliament, so that the idea of the Democrats sustaining a Conservative government (even one led by Mrs Thatcher's successor) becomes, as Neil Kinnock might say, 'untenable'. This would also encourage tactical voting against the Conservatives, especially by Labour voters, to offset the redefection from the Democrats to the Tories of the Tory protest vote. Many Labour supporters at the last election may have been deterred from voting tactically for second-place Alliance candidates by Dr Owen's apparent willingness to contemplate deals with Mrs Thatcher.

A popular front, whether formal or informal, is the only plausible alternative to transforming the Labour Party into something else. The electorate may have become more volatile over the years, but it is not volatile enough to contemplate an 8-percentage-point swing to Labour just for the sake of a bit of excitement. Labour's image as a faction-ridden class party has become deeply ingrained, and centre-party supporters have developed their distinctive loyalty and identity. As Peter Kellner pointed out in the *New Statesman* after the 1987 election, Labour has a stark choice: either it must change itself so radically and so successfully that it can appeal to over half of the centre-party voters itself, or it must do a deal with the centre party. 'The party must change more profoundly if it is to seek outright victory than if it is to embrace electoral reform and coalition rule,' Kellner wrote (19 June 1987).

A policy of openness towards one another would enable the opposition parties to disagree on unrelated policies while uniting on the values of collectivism. The implications of Curtice's analysis (see p. 156) are that a popular front should emphasise the collectivism of civil liberties and the welfare state, rather than that of collective action to achieve economic equality. Of course, the welfare state is egalitarian; collectivism itself, the belief that society as a whole has a responsibility to provide for all its members, is an indirectly egalitarian principle. But the emphasis would be on all-embracing collectives, rather than the sectional interests of trade unions.

Curtice's analysis also underlines the importance of stepping up the pace of *perestroika* in the trade union movement. What divides Labour supporters from Democrats more than anything else is the role of trade unions. (Defence policy splits both opposition parties as much as it divides them from each other.)[5] And the unions are the most immediate embodiment of the collectivist principle. Equality itself, as an abstract principle, is not such a divisive factor: put crudely, Labour supporters are not interested in equality as a principle, but in a better deal for the working class. Opinion poll questions which test 'pure' egalitarianism show how unpopular it is. In June 1985, MORI found that 60 per cent preferred 'a society which gives greater rewards for more skill, education and achievement', and only 23 per cent preferred 'one which emphasises similar incomes and rewards for everybody'.[6]

Equality in practice, however, as a principle of enablement, *is* popular – provided it is pursued through the 'all-inclusive' institutions of the welfare state rather than exclusively on behalf of the disadvantaged. So it makes sense to argue for equality by promoting the NHS and state schools, which benefit the middle class as well as the working class, rather than by promoting either the sectional interests of trade unions or a coalition of the dispossessed. Equality is not popular in the abstract, because it is associated with uniformity and holding people back, but can be pursued in the concrete as efficiency (putting people back to work) and fairness (progressive taxation).

It could be said that Labour's problem is that it represents organised labour and the Democrats' is that they don't. Trade unions are vital to the Labour Party as a politicising force, reinforcing the class base of the Labour vote (see Chapter 6). The spread of unionisation in white-collar jobs helped offset the shrinking of Labour's class base in the 1970s. The Democrats' social base, among the educated middle class, is much more fragile. But the 'domination' of the Labour Party by the trade unions remains a reason for not voting Labour often cited by ex-Labour or potential Labour voters, and is undoubtedly an obstacle to cooperation with the Democrats.

The trade union movement is undergoing reform, although the pace remains slow. The renewal of its internal democracies has mainly been forced on it by the Conservative government. But several unions have also modernised their image, trying to look more like professional service organisations than class battalions. Much fuss has been made by labour movement fundamentalists about the 'individualism' of providing services (especially financial services) to individual members, but this betrays an attachment to the forms of collectivism appropriate to a particular time, rather than a commitment to the principle.

The reform of the trade union movement will take as long as the realignment of the Left, and in the end the unions are bound to end up in a different relation to political parties from the present sclerotic set-up. What the shape of that settlement will be is well beyond the scope of this book. In 1987 the Labour Party introduced a complex form of one-member-one-vote (including local trade union votes) for the selection of MPs and candidates, and Labour has reluctantly accepted some of the Tory trade union laws, but the issue still seriously divides the non-Tory parties. The need for the Labour Party to democratise union block votes – which dominate party policy – is urgent. The block votes should represent the views of the trade union members who actually pay their political levy to the Labour Party – 'delegate democracy' is no longer appropriate in a time of mass literacy, mass communication and given people's greater self-confidence and desire for political participation.

Although support for the principles of collectivism has not been diminished by Mrs Thatcher's decade in power, it is not true that popular political values never change. The Labour Party still has to catch up with changes which occurred in the 1960s and 1970s. In those decades political values *did* change, to the advantage of the centre parties: people became more tolerant, liberal and self-confident in their demands to take part in politics.

There was a huge increase in the proportion of people who say they have done something to try to influence parliament. In a 1959 study only 6 per cent said they had 'ever done anything to try to influence an Act of Parliament'. A similarly worded question asked by the British Social Attitudes survey in 1986 found that 44 per cent had done something. More than half had done nothing more aggressive than sign a petition, but 20 per cent had contacted their MP, a government department or the media, gone on a protest or demonstration, or been active in a pressure group. As many as 11 per cent of the population have contacted their MP at some time.[7]

Arguments for collectivism

The arguments for collectivism have to be updated to appeal to more self-confident citizens, and to appeal across the party divide between the anti-Conservative forces. Labour shadow ministers Bryan Gould and Roy Hattersley have begun this process by demonstrating how Tory individualism offers freedom for only some individuals, and how cooperation and collective benefits provide a platform for the most extensive freedom for all.

Gould argues in his *Socialism and Freedom*:

> We must emphasise that the true concern of the socialist is *the individual* in society . . . This concern for each individual means that the socialist cannot tolerate a society in which the interests of only some individuals prevail, to the exclusion or devaluation of the interests of others. To the socialist, society is a co-operative enterprise in which the fact of participation is enough to provide an entitlement to equal respect and an equal share of social benefits. (pp. 105–6)

By starting from the individual, Gould helps reclaim the ideas of individual responsibility and individual achievement from Mrs Thatcher, and to show how individual ends can be achieved by collective means.

Very similar arguments are put forward by Hattersley in his *Choose Freedom*, which formed the basis of the Labour Party's *Statement of Aims and Values*, which declares: 'The true purpose of democratic socialism and, therefore, the true aim of the Labour

Party . . . is the protection and extension of individual liberty.'
Critics say it's boring, old fashioned and not very radical. But it
has the advantages of being simple, capable of uniting the non-Tory
forces in British politics and of being written. No alternative popular political philosophy for the Left has yet been successfully put
forward. And, far from being a sell-out to free-market capitalism, it
is in fact an effective weapon in the arguments *against* unrestrained
market forces. Hattersley argues that there is no point being free
if you are unable to exercise that freedom: so freedom for all
implies a collective responsibility to ensure that everyone has as
far as possible equal choices and equal opportunities. A large part
of the population, for instance, is denied access to the freedoms of
the property market – they do not possess the wherewithal to act
as free agents.

The idea of agency has a firm base in the popular idea of
'fundamental rights'. Even if someone only believes in equality of
opportunity, rather than equality of outcome, they must believe,
for example, that everyone must be healthy to be able to take
those opportunities in society. Asked if he believed in a free health
service, Mr N, a Wolverhampton foreman who voted SDP in 1987,
hesitated before saying: 'I think so. There are certain basic essentials
which everyone should have a right to.' Ms J, a Basildon Alliance
voter, said: 'I don't think you should have to pay to get something
as basic as health care.' The right to education, a decent home and
a basic income fall into the same category.

The inadequate basis of the Tory version of freedom is also
widely understood. For instance, public opinion is apparently very
evenly divided on the question of jumping the queue for NHS
treatment. When Gallup asked (see p.76): 'Do you think that it
is acceptable or unacceptable to jump the queue for treatment by
going privately?' forty-eight per cent said it was acceptable and 45
per cent that it was unacceptable (7 per cent didn't know). But
this leads to the contradiction at the heart of Tory individualism.
The 'freedom' that the Conservative Party offers is the freedom
to jump the queue, and it is self-defeating to offer that freedom
to everybody.

Real freedom involves eliminating the queue, an option not put
by Gallup to its respondents. Of course, the rationing of health care
can never be completely eliminated; as medical science advances
there will be new queues for new treatments. There do have to

be limits to the health care provided by the NHS, but it can't be argued that those limits have in general been reached when there is a huge consensus that more public money should be spent on the health service. For most people, the solution to the problems of the NHS *is* simply to spend more money. Gallup also asked whether the NHS needed more money or 'just a reorganisation': 72 per cent said 'more money', 22 per cent said 'reorganise'.

Cooperation and collective provision also enable the greatest possible number of people to help themselves and achieve independence. Many of the symbols of the new individualism are what Margaret Drabble called 'the offspring of fear'; they don't represent a desire for self-reliance and independence, but simply a fear of other people engendered by a divided society. 'Private health insurance, private hospitals, burglar alarms, barbed wire, guard dogs, fortress architecture – these are the fruits of our profit and progress,' she wrote in her *Case for Equality*.[8]

Self-help and independence are not – necessarily – Tory values, as David Blunkett pointed out (p. 18). The main way in which most people help themselves and achieve independence is work, which is precisely what has been denied the dependent minority by the economic policy of this government, a government which then has the cheek to complain of the 'dependency culture' it has created.

But tackling unemployment requires spending a lot of money on public works and proper training, and the political commentators want to know where the money is coming from. People may like Labour's policies on unemployment, schools and the NHS, they say, but they don't think the party can manage the economy well enough to produce the cash. They quote opinion polls like Marplan's for Channel 4's *A Week in Politics* (27 April 1988). It showed big majorities in favour of Labour's policy of real increases in spending on health and education, and widespread pessimism about whether standards in the NHS and state schools would get better in the next few years (only 18 per cent thought they would get better). Nor did most people think that Labour would be inefficient in running education or the NHS: asked if people would get less value for money from education services, 31 per cent agreed, but 41 per cent disagreed. However, when asked if the economy would be too weak under Labour to provide money for education and the NHS, more people agreed (42 per cent) than disagreed (33 per cent).

And indeed it is true that the voters don't trust Labour to handle the economy. But it is not true that the opposition parties do not have convincing economic policies between them. The electorate *does* believe that there is an alternative to Thatcherite economic policies. At the last election the economic policies of Labour and the Alliance were similar, and sharply differentiated from Conservative policy. And 57 per cent of the electorate voted for them. More specifically, in 1984–5 an average of 55 per cent of the population agreed that 'it is possible to have more people in jobs *and* low inflation at the same time', and only 22 per cent disagreed (*The Gallup Survey of Britain*, p. 113). The problem comes back to the machinery of politics, not the winning of arguments.

The ideas of the 'New Right' captured much of the political classes, not because they won the arguments but because Mrs Thatcher had captured control of the machinery of 'elective dictatorship', and because her opponents were demoralised by electoral defeat. But the New Right has failed dismally to win the arguments outside the closed world of Westminster and the Murdoch-led media. (Even in that closed world the fashion for monetarism – the specific theory of the money supply – passed almost as quickly as that for Adam Ant and the New Romantics among followers of pop music.)

Former Home Secretary Leon Brittan astutely observed that Conservative governments are concerned with what works: 'If it stopped working you might find that the ideological support for what it is doing is fairly skin deep' (BBC World Service, *People and Politics*, 16 April 1988). Other Conservatives have also begun to realise this, and Kenneth Baker, Douglas Hurd and Michael Heseltine have all tried to lay claim to a form of Toryism that is more soundly based on popular values of cooperation and social justice. Baker and Hurd have stressed the need to encourage a greater sense of social responsibility that goes beyond Mrs Thatcher and Nigel Lawson's exhortations to give generously to charity flag days. And Heseltine has advocated more government intervention in depressed urban areas and in the free market in helicopters, among other things.

From such clues it is possible dimly to make out the shape of post-Thatcherite Conservatism. Whatever its details, it obviously represents a move back towards collectivism. But, although the New Wets would like greater social cohesion, the adhesives they favour are the ties of hierarchy and the family rather than those of common citizenship. And why should the electorate vote for Tory collectivism when they could have the real thing, if only the opposition could get its act together?

A change of heart

Since the 1987 election, Margaret Thatcher's government has begun to seem like an 'old regime'; there has been a growing awareness of the gulf between the government's values and the people's values.

In part, this has been caused by the built-in backlash of Mrs Thatcher's politics. In the early Thatcher years, anxieties about the state of the health service, schools and streets, about crime and anti-social behaviour, were deferred. The promise was that once the government had knocked the economy into shape, these things would be attended to. The promise was that once the much neglected process of wealth creation was under way again, money would be spent on all the desirable things that the opinion polls show people want. If people kept their heads down, worked hard and let market forces reward virtue, they would get the better hospitals, schools and shining future they wanted.

Instead, they got the 1988 Budget, which gave top-rate income tax payers a 50 per cent rise in take-home pay for doing nothing. The richest one-twentieth of the population got a 20p tax bonus for every pound of their income over about £50,000 a year (the top rate was cut from 60p to 40p in the pound).

Steadily rising living standards for the majority of people in work had sustained the Conservatives at the polls against a divided opposition in 1983 and 1987. But, just at the point when many of those who had given the Conservatives the benefit of the doubt were beginning to realise that their standard of living was not *solely* a question of cash in pocket, Nigel Lawson stuffed the pockets of an already excessively privileged minority. It was bad politics, because it so clearly insulted the feeling that the government had gone too far in favouring the enrichment of individuals at the expense of collective advancement. And, to take one specific example, it was in the face of near unanimity outside the Downing Street court faction that the National Health Service needed at least £1 billion in order to keep up with reasonable and modest expectations.

167

People were becoming more aware that their standard of living had something to do with the state of the society and the environment in which they lived. Apart from money, there is also 'quality of life', which includes a sense that other people are well looked after, that the streets are clean and public spaces cared for. For many people, the Conservatives had delivered on the cash element of their standard of living, but because material standards for so many have been rising so steadily since 1982, the dashing of expectations of a higher quality of life has been all the greater.

Even Mrs Thatcher herself shows occasional subliminal signs of recognising the problem, as in this revealingly incoherent lecture delivered to *Woman* magazine (4 June 1988): 'Riches are not money. Or let me say, not only money. The greatest riches of all are a good family, which you can get at all income groups, and a good education. These are far more important than being born into a family which has a good deal of money.'

As has been seen, for the vast majority of the population education can only be provided collectively. Of course, the radical Right could do something about that, by privatising the whole education system, or introducing vouchers. But in the meantime, the 1988 Budget did not enable the vast majority of people to buy their children a better education. Nor could they buy cleaner streets, traffic-free roads or a less polluted environment. The limits of individualism had been reached.

Beneath the surface, other less explicitly political but equally significant changes in people's attitudes were also taking place. Attitudes to environmental issues continued to change after the Chernobyl accident in 1986. Fears about nuclear waste disposal were heightened and then overlaid with concern about toxic waste, the ozone layer, the greenhouse effect warming the atmosphere, dying seals and serried ranks of starter homes in the green belt. So much so that Mrs Thatcher went green in September 1988, saying: 'The government espouses the concept of sustainable economic development.' The whole point about sustainable economic development, of course, being that it requires society as a whole to restrain market forces, so that one generation's pursuit of higher living standards doesn't destroy the economic base for the next generation.

Attitudes to work have also changed since the 1987 election. Research by Gould Mattinson in July and August 1988 revealed a sense that work was less enjoyable, and that longer hours were diminishing the quality of life. Men as well as women wanted more time with their families. This was confirmed by British Telecom's decision – on the strength of market research – to base an advertising campaign on the idea of freeing people to spend more time at home: 'Married to the Boss' and 'Are You Becoming a Stranger at Home?'

Gould Mattinson also detected a shift in favour of the principle of trade unionism. A feeling of being under greater pressure at work led to a greater willingness to join trade unions. Whereas earlier research found young people especially were dismissive of unions, saying they meant nothing to them and had nothing to offer them, young people had come to regard trade union membership as self-evidently a good thing and necessary for the protection of their interests at work.

The Zeebrugge, King's Cross and Piper Alpha disasters also served to remind people of unions' role in pressing for safety measures against considerations of cost.

The British Telecom campaign is not the only example of advertising reflecting changing attitudes. In 1987, the marketing industry faithfully reflected the individualist fashion, with famous advertisements for British Airways, Pirelli, Vauxhall Cavalier and Volkswagen which celebrated selfish, competitive and acquisitive behaviour (the British Airways advertisement featured business executives 'fixing' a rival by arranging an overnight flight for him before an important meeting). But in April 1988 the advertising agency KHBB produced its forecast of consumer trends in the 1990s: *The Dawn of Us-ism*. After the fashion for Me-ism in the 1960s, and for 'rampant survivalism' in the 1980s, said KHBB, the question posed for the next decade will be 'Where are we all going (together)?' The agency, whose clients include the Prudential, Carlsberg and Saab, predicted that 'affluent altruism' is the wave of the future. 'In a world which is constantly changing and constantly being affected by the ravages of pollution, environmental decay, the Aids virus, consumer overload and ever-expanding choice, the need for group responsibility and group caring is fast becoming much less easy to sidestep,' KHBB argued.

No sooner had this forecast appeared than the insurance company Standard Life launched an advertising campaign featuring a single steel wire being twisted together with others to form a strong cable. The slogan was 'We're better off together' – but it could just as well have been 'Unity is Strength'.

Band Aid and Live Aid charity concerts were important precursors of affluent altruism, but part of their significance was that many of their supporters felt that their contributions were puny and poorly co-ordinated compared with what a government could achieve on behalf of the people collectively.

So, far from there being a New Individualism in popular political values, the politics of the 1990s are likely to be shaped by a reaffirmation of collectivism, and a concern for the environment – a concern which can be expressed individually but which inevitably requires collective action. Recent trends also suggest unmet demands for greater equality for women and for more meaningful democracy. Which suggests a politics for the 1990s which restores the balance between the public and private qualities of people's standard of living.

The post-Thatcherite consensus does exist, at the level of popular values and at the level of formal political philosophy. But neither the Labour Party nor the Democrats are yet very good at making that dual consensus vivid. They lack the 'Big Idea', or the political vision to set against the apparent clarity of Mrs Thatcher's prospectus. But many people do have in their mind's eye a vision, perhaps a little blurred, of a 'better society', in which public space is as meaningful, friendly and cared for as the private space of the home. It is a vision imbued with civic pride, where public service is an elevated motive, and where efficiency is pursued as much for collective benefit and collective pride as for individual gain.

'Collectivism' is not a good rallying cry, it's true. It reeks of the past. But Mrs Thatcher managed to update the decrepit ideas of classical economics and the brutal values of the Victorian period. On the other hand, socialism is not such a bad word. After all, more people want 'a mainly socialist society in which public interests and a more controlled economy are important' (49 per cent) than 'a mainly capitalist society in which private interests and free enterprise are most important' (43 per cent), according to MORI in June 1988.

The fashion for affluent altruism offers the Left the chance to leapfrog Thatcherite individualism, and deliver to the whole country what Thatcherism promises half of it – freedom. The Left has no choice: it has already been leapfrogged by Thatcherism claiming to be the realisation of the idealism of the 1960s, with its annexation of the slogan 'Power to the People' in the 1987 election campaign. And by its claim to deliver what Labour Party radicalism promised but failed to deliver in the 1970s – with Mrs Thatcher's annexation at the 1987 Tory party conference of Labour's 1974 manifesto promise of an 'irreversible shift of . . . power in favour of working people and their families' (although she significantly left out the 'wealth and'). But the Left can also deliver what Conservatism never can, and that is a better society – an entity, good or bad, which doesn't exist according to Mrs Thatcher.

The effects of Mrs Thatcher's media-manufactured dominance are not impossible to reverse; on the contrary, far from the Thatcher Revolution constituting an 'irreversible' shift in values, a final break with the post-war consensus, its achievements in redefining the politics of the possible actually show the way for a much more radical leftward shift than might have previously been thought possible. If Mrs Thatcher can do all this in the name of values that are inimical to those of the people, consider what a radical left-wing 'revolution' could achieve, going with the grain of other, more generous, facets of British people's values.

Appendix 1: Questionnaire

IDENTIFICATION QUESTIONS

Did you vote in the General Election this [last] year?

If yes: which party did you vote for?

If not Labour: have you ever voted Labour?

If yes: when was the last time?

Most people see themselves as belonging to a social class. Which of these would you say you belong to? (Middle, upper working, working, poor, don't know/none.)

And which social class would you say your parents belonged to when you started primary school?

MAIN INTERVIEW

(Working-class or upper working-class former Labour voters only.)

What was the most important thing that made you decide to change your vote? When did you decide?

How likely is it that you might vote Labour again in the future?

Do you vote for the party that you think will be best for you [and your family], or best for the country as a whole? (Or is it not possible to separate them?)

Why do you bother to vote at all?

Does the way you vote have anything to do with right and wrong [with morality] or is it just to do with your financial interests?

Should it be the government's responsibility to reduce income differences between rich and poor?

Thinking of yourself five years ago, are you now better off/worse off/about the same?

If better off, is that because you [your family] have worked hard/the whole country is doing better/you have been lucky?

And in the future? Say in five years' time, do you expect to be better off/worse off/about the same as now?

How easy is it to get to the top in Britain today? Is it easier than ten years ago?

Have the chances of working-class people getting to the top improved?

QUESTIONNAIRE

THE HEALTH SERVICE

Do you think private health care damages/takes resources away from the NHS?

Do you believe in the guiding philosophy behind the NHS (i.e. free health care for all according to need)?

(If without private health insurance): Would you have private health insurance if you could afford it? Do you know how much it costs?

Do you think it is realistic to try to improve the NHS so that no one would want private health care?

Do you think it is easy enough to change your GP [family doctor] if you're dissatisfied? Would you rather have a private family doctor if you could afford it?

EDUCATION

If you could afford it [and if you had children], would you want [have wanted] to send your children to a private school? If yes, why?

If your children were at a private school do you think you would have more say over what is taught than in a state school?

What is the most important thing when choosing schools? [Exam results/discipline/Christian teaching?]

Are there too many permissive/trendy subjects being taught in schools?

HOUSING

Why do people want to own their own homes? Do you think it's better for people to own their own homes? Should home ownership be subsidised by the government?

Are council house sales a good idea? What about the problem of there being fewer council houses left? Should it be the responsibility of the government or local councils to provide housing?

(Home owners): does owning your own home make you feel part of the 'property owning democracy' [i.e. that the government talks about]?

SHARE OWNERSHIP

(Share owners): does owning shares make you feel part of the 'share owning democracy' [i.e. that the government talks about]?

(Non-share-owners): would you want to own shares if you could afford it?

Has the crash [last year] changed your mind about owning shares? Do you think shares are a good investment? Is it better for the economy if ordinary people invest in shares?

Does the small shareholder have any power over the company? Should small shareholders get together to have more influence?

Should monopolies like British Telecom, British Gas, electricity and the water industry be state owned? If not, should the government control their prices? And profits?

Should people own shares in the company they work for?

TRADE UNIONS

(Trade union members): Why are you in a union? (If 'have to be' or 'closed shop': do you want to be in it anyway?) Does being in a union make a difference if you are unfairly dismissed, wrongly accused of something by your employer or have your conditions of work changed?

Is it ever worth going on strike? Do you think unions in general are/your union is too ready to go on strike? Have you ever been on strike? If yes, did you agree with it? Do you think workers get better pay and conditions by getting together or by working hard on their own?

UNEMPLOYMENT

Is it the government's duty to provide a decent income to the unemployed?

Do you or your children feel threatened by unemployment?

What is (are) the most important achievement(s) in your life?

Do you think of yourself as a religious person?

Interviewees were also asked a series of classification questions about their occupation, union membership, family, housing, share ownership and private health insurance.

Appendix 2: Interviews Index

Gould Mattinson post-election interviews

Telephone interviews and groups discussions carried out by Gould Mattinson and Associates, June to October 1987 (summary report commissioned for this book). Interviewees mostly social grade C1/C2, mostly defected from Labour in 1983 or 1987.

Our own interviews

Face-to-face interviews in the home carried out by Jane Ratford and John Rentoul. Lapsed Labour (except Scotland), self-described as working class except two middle-class women.

A–F: Putney, South London, November/December 1987 (Jane Ratford).

G–K: Basildon, Essex, December 1987 (Jane Ratford).

L–P: (plus Q–T short interviews): Wolverhampton, West Midlands, December 1987 (John Rentoul).

U–Z: Glasgow, February 1988 (John Rentoul).

Mr A

Job:	Office services clerk, supervising two people
Age:	About 30
Family:	Single
Vote:	Alliance in 1987; now thought of himself as closer to Labour
Class:	Working class
Union:	Member
Home:	Council flat
Shares:	Yes
Health insurance:	No

Mr B

Job:	Tool room universal grinder in car parts company, supervising three people

175

Age:	About 30
Family:	Wife a local council manual worker, two children under school age
Vote:	Didn't vote in 1987: 'The leaders of the opposition parties did not seem strong enough to lead the country. Although the Conservatives do have a strong leader, I do not agree with their policies.' Also disliked the 'left-wing' Peter Hain, Labour's candidate in Putney. Thought of himself as closer to Labour and voted Labour before (1983).
Class:	Working class
Union:	Non-member
Home:	Council flat, rent free with wife's job
Shares:	No
Health insurance:	No

Mr C

Job:	Retired superintendent of a public institution, responsible for 300 manual staff
Age:	Old age pensioner
Family:	Wife Ms C (interviewed jointly), no children
Vote:	Alliance in 1987; but still thought of himself as closer to Labour; previously a Labour voter (last in 1983). Another who disliked the 'left-wing' Peter Hain, the Labour candidate in Putney.
Class:	Working class
Union:	Former member
Home:	Council flat
Shares:	No
Health insurance:	No

Ms C

Job:	Retired, looked after the house
Age:	Old age pensioner
Family:	Husband Mr C (interviewed jointly), no children
Vote:	Labour, always
Class:	Working class
Union:	Not applicable
Home:	Council flat
Shares:	No

Health insurance: No

Mr D

Job: Painter-decorator and theatre worker, self-employed
Age: About 45
Family: Wife Ms D (interviewed separately), one child of school age; grown-up children by previous marriage
Vote: Conservative in 1987; last voted Labour in 1983.
Class: Working class
Union: Member
Home: Council house
Shares: No
Health insurance: Yes

Ms D

Job: Personal assistant to senior executive
Age: About 40
Family: Husband Mr D (interviewed separately), one child of school age
Vote: Conservative in 1987; last voted Labour in 1979
Class: Upper working class
Union: Non-member
Home: Council house
Shares: No
Health insurance: Yes

Mr E

Job: Bank clerk
Age: 60
Family: Wife Ms E (interviewed separately), grown-up children
Vote: Conservative in 1987; not a supporter but would vote Conservative again; last voted Labour 1970 or 1974.
Class: Upper working class
Union: Former member
Home: House owned outright
Shares: No
Health insurance: No

Ms E

Job: Retired nurse, supervising three people

Age:	60
Family:	Husband Mr E (interviewed separately), grown-up children
Vote:	Alliance in 1987; not a supporter but would vote Alliance again; last voted Labour 1970 or 1974
Class:	Working class, of upper working-class parents
Union:	Former member Royal College of Nursing (non-TUC affiliated)
Home:	House owned outright
Shares:	No
Health insurance:	No

Ms F

Job:	Unemployed/looking after the home; former supervisor for a cleaning contractor, 24 hours a week, supervising six people
Age:	About 40
Family:	Single, one child below school age, two at school and one grown up
Vote:	Conservative in 1987; would now vote Labour; last voted Labour in 1983
Class:	Poor, of working–class parents
Union:	Never a member
Home:	Council house
Shares:	No
Health insurance:	No

Mr G

Job:	Machine operator supervising one or two trainees, recently unemployed for three years
Age:	57
Family:	Wife an advertising salesperson, one school-age child
Vote:	Conservative in 1987; has voted Labour, last in local council elections
Class:	Working class
Union:	Former member (shop steward, Transport and General Workers Union)
Home:	Council house, rented
Shares:	No
Health insurance:	No

Mr H

Job:	Lorry driver, employee
Age:	Late 20s
Family:	Wife a bank clerk, one child under and one of school age
Vote:	Conservative in 1987; not a supporter but would vote Conservative again; last voted Labour in 1979
Class:	Working class
Union:	Member
Home:	House owned with mortgage, not bought from council (was council tenant for three years)
Shares:	No
Health insurance:	No

Ms J

Job:	Library assistant, 18 hours a week
Age:	About 40
Family:	Husband a manual worker in brewery, two children, 17 and 21 at home, one older
Vote:	Alliance in 1987; would vote Alliance again: 'I liked the way they were hoping to do things'; last voted Labour in 1966: 'I have very fond memories of the Wilson years; I could see myself voting Labour again if they went back to what the old Labour Party stood for.'
Class:	Middle class, of working-class parents
Union:	Former member
Home:	House owned with a mortgage, bought from the council five years ago, having been council tenants for fourteen years
Shares:	Yes
Health insurance:	Yes, through husband's employer

Mr K

Job:	Wages clerk, public sector
Age:	About 50
Family:	Wife a supermarket cashier, two school-age children
Vote:	Didn't vote in 1987: 'I finally came to the conclusion that the outcome of the election depended on 70 per cent of the population who didn't have a clue what they were voting for. I didn't wish to continue as part of such

a futile system. Labour changed their policies from one way to another to try to become popular. I never agree with anyone doing that. [And] there were some people in the party, the left wing, who were going in a ridiculous direction. But at other times it was trying to become all things to all men, which never works. But, basically, it was realising the outcome of the election depended on a populace led by propaganda and advertising. There was no hope that any thinking people in the country could produce a good government. It's unlikely that I will ever vote Labour again, or indeed ever vote again.' Thinks of himself as closer to Labour, and last voted Labour in 1983.

Class:	Working class
Union:	Member
Home:	Council house
Shares:	No
Health insurance:	No

Mr L

Job:	Unemployed, recently made redundant as factory store-man
Age:	About 50
Family:	Wife Ms L (interviewed jointly), one child of school age
Vote:	Conservative in 1987; previously Labour, last in 1983
Class:	Working class
Union:	Member
Home:	Council house
Shares:	No
Health insurance:	No

Ms L

Job:	Looking after the house
Age:	About 50
Family:	Husband Mr L (interviewed jointly), one child of school age
Vote:	Conservative in 1987: 'Conservatives mainly stick to what they say they are going to do'; previously Labour, last in 1983

Class:	Working class
Union:	Not applicable
Home:	Council house
Shares:	No
Health insurance:	No

Ms M

Job:	Retired primary school teacher
Age:	Old age pensioner
Family:	Husband a retired maintenance fitter, grown-up children
Vote:	Conservative in 1987; last voted Labour in 1964, consistent Conservative since: 'Labour would not do anything about immigration.'
Class:	Working class
Union:	Former member
Home:	Owned, not bought from the council
Shares:	Yes
Health insurance:	No

Mr N

Job:	Foreman in engineering company
Age:	Late 30s
Family:	Wife a full-time skilled manual worker, two children of school age
Vote:	Social Democratic Party in 1987: 'it came with age a bit; it was the lack of democracy in the two main parties, too much extremism'; last voted Labour in 1983 (uncertain); also had voted Conservative, 'when they were more moderate'.
Class:	Upper working class, of parents 'almost the same, although they owned a business, a few shops; upper working class with middle-class ideals, which they've passed on to me'.
Union:	Member
Home:	Owned, not bought from council
Shares:	Yes (unit trusts)
Health insurance:	No

Ms O

Job:	Full-time student, former nurse
Age:	About 35
Family:	Husband a hospital technician, two school-age children
Vote:	Liberal in 1987; voted Liberal in by-election of local council election once previously, but consistent Labour before that; last voted Labour in 1983: 'because Labour was going too left wing'; not likely to vote Labour again, 'not the way things are going'.
Class:	Middle class
Union:	Former member
Home:	Council house
Shares:	No
Health insurance:	Yes

Mr P

Job:	Semi-skilled manual worker in a factory
Age:	About 30
Family:	Married, no children
Vote:	Conservative in 1987; last voted Labour in 1979: 'before they started making arses of themselves; she makes it easier for people to better themselves – you get rewarded if you work hard; I'm not very interested in politics, I'm only interested in doing a hard day's work'; 'very unlikely' to change.
Class:	Working class
Union:	Member, Transport and General Workers Union
Home:	House owned, not bought from council (never been a council tenant)
Shares:	'No comment'
Health insurance:	Yes

Mr Q

Job:	N/A
Age:	35
Family:	Married, two young children
Vote:	Conservative; last voted Labour 1974
Class:	Working class (but 'I have bettered myself')
Union:	N/A
Home:	Rented from council
Shares:	N/A

Health insurance: N/A

Mr R

Job: Metal mechanic

Age: About 30

Family: Single, living with mother

Vote: Conservative, always, 'except when I'd just left school, I voted Labour, before I knew better; nearly voted National Front once'.

Class: Working class

Union: 'Metal mechanics union'

Home: Owned with mortgage

Shares: No

Health insurance: No

Mr S

Job: Truck driver

Age: 45–50

Family: Married with four sons, three working, one at school

Vote: Labour (a little uncertainly) in 1987, SDP in 1983, and Labour consistently before that. 'Didn't like the Labour leader at the time. Foot it was.' So you think Neil Kinnock is all right? 'Not really.'

Class: Working class

Union: Transport and General Workers

Home: Owned with mortgage, 'bought from council this twelve months'

Shares: Yes

Health insurance: No

Mr T

Job: Skilled fitter, aerospace

Age: 40–45

Family: Divorced

Vote: Conservative; 'always have; the family always have voted Conservative'.

Class: Working class

Union: AEU, paying political levy ('it's compulsory really')

Home:	Owned with mortgage, former council tenant ('only when I first got married twenty-two years ago')
Shares:	N/A
Health insurance:	N/A

Mr U

Job:	Retired engineer
Age:	Old age pensioner
Family:	Married, two grown-up children
Vote:	Labour, always. 'But it's not automatic; I have thought about it and I always might do something different.'
Class:	Working class
Union:	Former member, AEU.
Home:	Rented from council
Shares:	No
Health insurance:	No

Ms V

Job:	Looking after home
Age:	50
Family:	Widow of self-employed draughtsman, two grown-up daughters
Vote:	Labour, always, although 'cross enough to abstain' in local elections over school closures
Class:	Working class
Union:	No
Home:	Owned outright, worth £100,000
Shares:	Yes
Health insurance:	No

Ms W

Job:	Retired, looking after home
Age:	Old age pensioner
Family:	Widow of motor mechanic (ex-services, war widow), two grown-up daughters
Vote:	SDP in 1983 and 1987; Labour before: 'Fed up with Labour, the carry-on, the fighting within the party. They need to do very well before I would think of voting for them.'
Class:	Working class

Union:	No
Home:	Rented from war veterans' charity
Shares:	No
Health insurance:	No

Mr Y

Job:	Retired company accountant
Age:	Old age pensioner
Family:	Single
Vote:	Labour, always
Class:	Working class
Union:	No
Home:	Rented
Shares:	No
Health insurance:	No

Ms Z

Job:	Looking after the home
Age:	25–30
Family:	Married to soldier (non-voter), two pre-school children
Vote:	SDP in 1987; 'I was out of the country before, the last time. No, it was SNP before, in the 1970s.'
Class:	Working class
Union:	No
Home:	Army house
Shares:	No
Health insurance:	No

Gould Mattinson group discussions

Two group discussions in Roehampton, South London, 29 February 1988. All recruited as C1, C2 lapsed Labour voters, voting Conservative or Alliance 1987. One with eight women (five Conservative, two Alliance and one Labour tactical voter), one with six men (five Conservative and one Alliance).

The women

Di

Job:	Librarian
Family:	Husband a manager of a garage, skilled mechanic
Vote:	Conservative in 1987; last voted Labour in 1966; has voted Liberal

Lynn

Job: Looks after the home

Family: two school-age children, two much older. Husband painter-decorator.

Vote: Conservative in 1987; last voted Labour probably in 1979 ('1981'). 'Basically I voted selfishly because I think that if the Labour got in, in this particular area, they don't want you to buy your property, so they would make it harder to buy your property. I don't really go into it deeply, like National Health and things like that. [Just property?] Well, no. Basically I wouldn't say that I'm for any of them. I think they all change when they get in. There's not any one group that's been in that's really done a lot of good. So I'm not really for any of them.'

Carol

Job   Domestic and school meals supervisor, part-time.

Age: 36

Family: Husband a brewery engineer

Vote: Claimed at the end of the discussion to have voted Labour in 1987 ('I voted for better education. There's no books in their school, they're sharing books'), although recruited as an SDP voter, which she later confirmed. Has also voted Conservative. Last voted Labour 1974.

Wendy

Job: Nurse, part-time

Age: About 40

Family: Husband an engineer in limb-fitting supply hospital; one child.

Vote: SDP in 1987; last voted Labour in 1974. 'I was a little bit undecided, really. I felt, after having voted SDP, it was a wasted vote. I can quite understand people that don't vote, because they don't necessarily agree with any of them. I know a lot of people think they're being apathetic, but I can understand how they feel.'

Janet

Job: School kitchen assistant

Age: About 40–44

Family: Husband an ambulance driver; one child at home.

Vote: Conservative in 1987; claimed to have last voted Labour in 1983. 'I'd do it again, even though I don't agree with a lot of things she's doing. I don't think I've got much choice.'

INTERVIEWS INDEX

Sylvia

Job: Business studies student, full-time; Yugoslav citizen

Family: Husband landscape gardener/groundsman for council

Vote: Labour supporter voting tactically for Liberals in Richmond in 1987; previously always Labour.

Jane

Job: Nursery school worker

Age: 36–40

Family: Husband a warehouse manager

Vote: Conservative in 1987; last voted Labour in 1979. 'Basically I think all my family . . . it's always been put into to me to vote for Labour, and I did vote Conservative because I didn't feel the other party was strong enough, and I agreed on some of the Conservatives' policies. But I'm not quite so happy about what's going on now. I think they're doing things now that they haven't quite mentioned in the manifesto. I knew they were going to do changes, but not quite like this. I don't think they said they were going to collapse ILEA totally. To be perfectly honest, I voted for her, but if I'd have realised what she was going to do . . . I cannot *believe* what she's going to do on education. I think it's appalling.'

Ann

Job: Home help

Age: 40–44

Family: Husband a cabinet-maker in a factory; two children, one grandchild.

Vote: Conservative in 1987; claimed to be Labour until 1987. 'We voted Conservative purely because we're buying our own home, and my daughter is buying her home. And we thought that if Labour gets in, I mean at our ages, we don't stand a chance of buying private, so this was the big chance for us.'

The men

Tony

Job: Builder-decorator, ex-greengrocer, own business

Vote: Conservative in 1987; voted Labour once, 1974 ('time of last mining strike').

187

Brian

Job: Police forensic scientist

Vote: SDP in 1987; claimed to have last voted Labour in 1983.

Jack

Job: Carpet fitter, self-employed

Vote: Conservative in 1987; last voted Labour 1979; also claims SDP vote (presumably in 1983), although a fairly strong Conservative. 'I voted Conservative because of Margaret Thatcher.'

Jonathan

Job: Landscape gardener (made redundant six months ago)

Age: 44

Family: One unemployed son at home

Vote: Conservative in 1987; last voted Labour 1979. Softer line. 'You couldn't vote for the last Labour government.'

Hugh

Job: Electrician for a private institution

Vote: Conservative in 1987; last voted Labour in 1979. Softer line again. 'I only voted for the Conservatives because there was nothing better, really. I've voted Labour all my life.'

David

Job: Housing officer for Wandsworth Borough Council

Vote: Conservative in 1987; claimed to have last voted Labour 'before Harold Wilson came to power', which would be 1959, when he was at most 15. Earliest feasible election is 1966 when he could have been 22, possibly 1970, 'before Harold Wilson came to power' for a second time. Also claims to have voted SDP, which must have been 1983, despite being a hard-line Tory.

All 36–44 parents; all working class except Sylvia ('I don't see myself in British classes'), Janet who was undecided, Geoff who was in between and David, 'middle working'.

Notes

1 The 'Thatcher Revolution'

1 Publishing details of all books referred to in the text are given in the Bibliography, p. 199
2 George Bernard Shaw, *A Short History of the Fabian Society*, 1892.
3 Quoted by Mark Franklin, *The Decline of Class Voting in Britain*, p. 162.
4 R. E. Pahl and C. D. Wallace, 'Forms of Work and Privatisation on the Isle of Sheppey', in B. Roberts, R. Finnegan and D. Gallie (eds), *New Approaches to Economic Life*, Manchester University Press, 1987.
5 David Sanders, Hugh Ward and David Marsh, 'Government Popularity and the Falklands War: A reassessment', Essex Papers in Politics and Government No. 40, University of Essex, September 1986.
6 'The Love of Money', BBC Radio 4, 23 February 1988.
7 Nicholas Deakin, 'In Search of the Postwar Consensus', Welfare State Programme discussion paper 25, London School of Economics, February 1988, pp. 15, 17, 29, 30.
8 Sidney and Beatrice Webb, 'What is Socialism? II. A change of heart', *New Statesman*, 19 April 1913.
9 Alexis de Tocqueville, *Democracy in America*, 1835, Part II, chapter 27.
10 Anthony Heath, Roger Jowell and John Curtice, *How Britain Votes*, pp. 16–18.
11 Jeremy Bentham, *An Introduction to the Principles of Morals and Legislation* edited by J. H. Burns and H. L. A. Hart, Athlone Press, 1970, p. 12.
12 In particular an article by Stuart Hall in *Marxism Today*, January 1979, and *The Politics of Thatcherism*, 1983, edited by Stuart Hall and Martin Jacques, pp. 25–6.

2 Overview

1 Bo Särlvik and Ivor Crewe, *Decade of Dealignment*, pp. 190–1.
2 Anthony Heath, Roger Jowell and John Curtice, *How Britain Votes*, pp. 132–8; the equality questions were on nationalisation and redistribution, the liberal questions were on the death penalty, abortion, and sex and race equality.

3 *British Social Attitudes: The 1986 Report*, p. 52.
4 *British Social Attitudes: The 1987 Report*, p. 171.
5 *British Social Attitudes: The 1986 Report*, p. 48, *British Social Attitudes: The 1987 Report*, p. 174 (excluding the last three items).
6 The third-party vote is not as classless as is often thought, however; it is less class-specific than the Labour or Tory vote, but is still quite middle class, and so it is actually more true that the Tory vote has suffered from (absolute rather than relative) class dealignment than that the Labour vote has.
7 *How Britain Votes*, pp. 28f; Ivor Crewe, 'On the Death and Resurrection of Class Voting', *Political Studies*, 34, 1986; Heath, Jowell and Curtice, 'Trendless Fluctuation: A Reply to Crewe', *Political Studies*, 35, June 1987.
8 *Decade of Dealignment*, p. 170; *How Britain Votes*, pp. 134, 203; *British Social Attitudes: The 1986 Report*, p. 241. It was asked in a different form in 1974 and 1979.

'Redistributing income and wealth in favour of ordinary working people' [in a list of things that it was important that the government should or should not do]

	Oct 1974 BES %	1979 BES %
The government should	54	52
The government should not	27	26
Doesn't matter/Don't know	19	22

'Income and wealth should be redistributed towards ordinary working people'

	Apr/ May 1983 BES %	Dec 1985 BSA %	May 1985 G %	Apr/ May 1986 G %	May 1987 BSA %	Nov 1987 G %	Average 1983-87 %
Agree	47	41	60	61	45	57	52
Disagree	37	28	24	25	33	28	29
Not sure/Don't know	16	29*	16	14	22*	15	19

* Neither/Don't know

(BES: British Election Studies; BSA: British Social Attitudes surveys; G: Gallup.)

9 *How Britain Votes*, p. 38. According to Gallup, the proportion agreeing that 'the rich get richer, the poor get poorer' after each year's Budget rose from 66 per cent in 1980 to 84 per cent in 1988.

	%
March 1980	66
March 1981	70
March 1982	75
March 1983	74
March 1985	75
March 1986	81
March 1987	79
March 1988	84

(1980–5: *The Gallup Survey of Britain*, p. 124; 1986–8: Gallup Political Index; in a list of things 'people have said about the government's taxation policy'.)

However, when similar questions are asked at other times of the year, the proportion agreeing has been around 70 per cent.

	%
November 1979	71
March (pre-Budget) 1981	69
February 1985	77
November 1986	69
February 1987	70
April 1987	72
May 1987	68
January 1988	71

(1979: format as above, *The Gallup Survey of Britain*, p. 124; 1981: *The Gallup Report 1981*, p. 75; 1985: format as above in a list of things 'people have told us they felt from time to time', *The Gallup Survey of Britain*, p. 141; 1986 to 1988: percentage agreeing that 'the rich are getting richer and the poor are getting poorer under this government', Gallup Political Index.)

10 Support for greater material equality is much higher if the statement is phrased 'It should be the government's responsibility to reduce income differences between the rich and poor' (72 per cent, 1986 British Social Attitudes, 69 per cent, Gallup, December 1985). Change 'rich and poor' to 'people with high incomes and those with low incomes' and support goes down to 59 per cent; change 'reduce income differences' back to 'redistribute income' and support falls to 43 per cent (both 1986 British Social Attitudes survey).

11 Gallup Political Index. For wording of the 1973 questions see p. 37; the 1987 question is 'the government should get rid of private education in Britain' (see also *The Gallup Survey of Britain*, p. 131).

12 *British Social Attitudes: The 1987 Report*, p. 254. No question about private schools was asked in the 1979 British Election Study. There appeared to be an increase in hostility to private schools between 1983 and 1985, with the proportion saying private education should *not* be got rid of falling from 70 per cent to 59

per cent (*How Britain Votes*, p. 18; *The Gallup Survey of Britain*, p. 131).

13 1974 (October) and 1979: *Decade of Dealignment*, p. 169; other figures from Gallup.

14 British Election Studies, quoted in *British Social Attitudes: The 1987 Report*, p. 58.

3 Education

1 Figures do not add up to 100 because of rounding. Note the very small sample: 304 parents of children aged 11–18 at state secondary schools or sixth-form colleges in a sample of 1,940 people aged 18 and over, MORI (*British Public Opinion*, October 1987, p. 5).

2 It's a nice political point, but it probably isn't true that middle-class childless socialists are the most hostile to private education. Twenty-one per cent of manual workers want to reduce or abolish private schools, as against 14 per cent of non-manual workers (*British Social Attitudes: The 1984 Report*, p. 117).

3 *British Social Attitudes: The 1984 Report*, p. 117, *The 1987 Report*, p. 210.

4 See note 1.

5 Before the introduction of comprehensive schools, between 20 and 25 per cent of each age cohort of children was creamed off by the Eleven Plus into grammar or other selective schools. This proportion varied between different education authorities, from as low as 14 per cent to 33 per cent (in Birmingham). The class division in the Eleven Plus was demonstrated by a study in Sheffield in the 1960s which found that six primary schools consistently had no children passing the Eleven Plus at all; another twenty schools had fewer than five passes each; while three primary schools in the middle-class districts had between 70 and 90 per cent of their pupils passing.

6 *The Guardian*, 9 February 1988. Marplan's sample size was 1,479, of whom 384 were parents with children currently at school: 16 per cent of them supported opting out, 70 per cent wanted to remain under local council control and 14 per cent didn't know or weren't sure.

7 The British Social Attitudes figures on racial prejudice are averages of 1983 and 1986; the figures on homosexuality are from the 1987 survey (*The 5th Report*, p. 74: that for adoption refers to male homosexuals; the figure for lesbians is 86 per cent).

8 British Social Attitudes survey 1987: 10 per cent of those who did not go to private school say there should be more of them, as against 17 per cent of those who did. The 13 per cent who did go to private school is a larger figure than the proportion of schoolchildren attending private schools, around 7 per cent, quoted on p. 37 because many

children go to state primary schools and only then to private secondary schools (and this is only partly offset by the fact that the private sector is overrepresented at sixth-form level).

9 Oddly enough, the three Rs originally *were* a magic formula. They were a Freemasons' device, a triangle with 'reading and writing' and 'reckoning and figuring' at the two bottom corners and 'wroughting and wrighting' at the top, according to Christopher Price, *New Statesman*, 18 September 1987.

4 Housing

1 *How Britain Votes*, p. 52; the marginality of the influence of housing tenure – over and above class – is confirmed by statistical analysis by Gordon Marshall and others, *Social Class in Modern Britain*, pp. 252–3.

5 Health Care

1 *British Social Attitudes: The 1984 Report*, p. 188, Q59b, and *The 1987 Report*, p. 209, Q61b (see also p. 210, Q62).
2 *British Social Attitudes: The 1984 Report*, p. 188, Q60, and *The 1987 Report*, p. 210, Q64.
3 British Social Attitudes 1986 survey (*The 1987 Report*, p. 209): 13.9 per cent; Gallup, March 1988: 13 per cent – note that some people are known to report having private health insurance when they haven't because of its social status.
4 Ralph Harris and Arthur Seldon, *Welfare Without the State*, p. 21. The full figures back to 1963 are as follows (for question wording see p. 83).

		1963	1965	1970	1978	1987
Health services						
A.	Better universal provision	41	32	29	20	30
B.	Concentrate on poor	24	25	24	18	19
C.	Allow contracting out	33	34	46	54	44
	Don't know	2	9	1	7	6
Education						
A.	Better universal provision	51	41	44	15	25
B.	Concentrate on poor	20	16	20	17	20
C.	Allow contracting out	27	32	35	60	48
	Don't know	2	11	2	8	6

6 Trade Unions

1 *Gallup Survey of Britain*, p. 145.
2 Gallup: there was an increase from 22 to 28 per cent in the proportion thinking they had 'a say' in their trade unions from February 1973 to May 1978. Gallup found no significant change in 'self influence' in respect of: government; banks, finance houses and building societies; shops; nationalised industries; newspapers. People felt they had less 'say' in: local councils; education; television (both BBC and ITV). And they felt they had more 'say' in: conditions at work; trade unions.
3 Forty-six per cent agree that 'employees need strong trade unions to protect their interests', 28 per cent disagree: average of 1985 and 1986 British Social Attitudes survey (*The 1986 Report*, p. 244, *The 1987 Report*, p. 252).
4 Quoted by John MacInnes, *Thatcherism at Work: Industrial Relations and Economic Change*, p. ix.

7 Share Ownership

1 John Hills, *New Statesman*, 13 March 1987. Total taxes (including rates and so on) as a percentage of GDP at factor cost. Different figures are produced by different methods of calculation; the government prefers to use the 'market prices' method as this gives lower figures for the tax take, but the trend is the same (up a lot and then down a bit).
2 The majority for further nationalisation was as follows (percentage points, negative figures indicate majority for more 'denationalisation').

1973	1974	1975	1976	1977	1978	1979	1980
+3	+7	−10	−17	−19	−15	−19	−21

1981	1982	1983	1984	1985	1986	1987
−21	−20	−20	−12	−9	−7	−4

All figures for the autumn of the relevant year, except summer 1973 and spring 1987.

8 Social Security

1 All three polls quoted in *British Social Attitudes: The 1987 Report*, p. 10: 1976 was a Eurobarometer survey by Gallup, 1983 was a MORI poll which asked a similar question with a similar choice of replies, and 1986 was the British Social Attitudes survey of that year.
2 Peter Taylor-Gooby, *British Social Attitudes: The 1987 Report*, p. 8. These questions were asked in face-to-face interviews and not in the self-completion questionnaire, and so may be slightly biased towards 'middle-class compassion', as respondents don't want to appear harsh to a strange interviewer.

3   Anthony Heath, Roger Jowell, John Curtice and Sharon Witherspoon, *British Election Study Follow-Up Interviews: End of Award Report*, Social and Community Planning Research, 1987, p. 28.
4   Ibid, pp. 24-5.
5   MORI, average for fourth quarter 1981: Liberal-SDP Alliance 38 per cent, Labour 28 per cent, Conservatives 27 per cent; Gallup: in October and December 1981 only 24 and 25 per cent were satisfied with Mrs Thatcher as prime minister (Harold Wilson was the previous holder of the Nadir Trophy with 27 per cent in May 1968), *The Gallup Report 1980*, pp. 168–85, and *The Gallup Report 1981*, p. 192.
6   Peter Jenkins, *Mrs Thatcher's Revolution*, p. 320

9   Prosperity

1   A statistically insignificant number of female manual workers earned £350 a week or more in April 1987; *Employment Gazette*, November 1987, p. 569.
2   *The Gallup Survey of Britain*, p. 127; Gallup Political Index. The proportion favouring the status quo, 18–25 per cent, and the don't knows, 5–7 per cent, didn't change much.
3   First column: Gallup/BBC 10–11 June 1987, 'Think of all the urgent problems facing the country at the present time. When you decided which way to vote which two issues did you personally consider most important?' Second column: Harris 10 June 1987, 'What are the two most important issues facing you and your family?'
4   Gallup. In June 1985, 22 per cent said 'better off', 26 per cent said 'no difference', 50 per cent said 'worse off' (*The Gallup Survey of Britain*, p. 140). Averaging September and October 1987, and March and April 1988, 27 per cent said 'better', 41 per cent 'same' and 31 per cent 'worse'.
5   Nick Morris and Ian Preston, 'Taxes, Benefits and the Distribution of Income 1968–83', *Fiscal Studies*, November 1986, and Institute for Fiscal Studies estimates of the effects of the 1988 Budget.
6   *How Britain Votes*, p. 38.
7   Speech to Conservative Council, Buxton, 19 March 1988.
8   Full-time men; the figures for full-time women were 20 per cent and 36 per cent; 'Trends in the Distribution of Earnings, 1973 to 1986', *Employment Gazette*, February 1988, Department of Employment, p. 76

10   Morality

1   John Robinson, *The Body: A Study of Pauline Theology*, 1952, quoted by Canon Eric James, *New Statesman*, 3 June 1988.

2 Speech made in Tamworth, February 1988, quoted in the *New Statesman* editorial, 15 April 1988.

3 Figures from Gallup except 1974 (October), 1979 and 1983 from the British Election Studies, *Decade of Dealignment*, p. 169, *How Britain Votes*, p. 136.

4 *British Social Attitudes: The 1987 Report*, p. 127. The 1981 figure from the European Value Systems Study carried out by Gallup.

5 *British Social Attitudes: The 1986 Report*, p. 166.

6 This is the only question wording that has been used consistently. Figures from Gallup except 1974 (October), 1979 and 1983 from the British Election Studies, *Decade of Dealignment*, p. 169, *How Britain Votes*, p. 136. British Social Attitudes surveys show a rise between 1983 and 1987 in the average percentage agreeing that abortion should be legal in various circumstances from 61 to 72 per cent (*The 5th Report*, p. 41).

7 *British Social Attitudes: The 1986 Report*, p. 152.

8 Adjusting for an average 2-point rise in intolerance of the nine other groups in the list: Gordon Heald and Robert Wybrow, *The Gallup Survey of Britain*, p. 169. The 1986 figures were 21 and 17 per cent respectively.

9 *British Social Attitudes: The 1984 Report*, pp. 196–7, and *British Social Attitudes: The 1987 Report*, pp. 211 and 225. The figures on the question of whether equal opportunities have gone too far are from the British Election Studies for 1974 (October), 1979 and 1983; the figures for 1978 and 1981 are from Gallup. Just to confuse matters further, British Social Attitudes surveys also found a 4-point decline in support for 'the idea of a law against racial discrimination' to 65 per cent and an equivalent rise in opposition to it to 32 per cent, between 1983 and 1986 (*British Social Attitudes: The 1984 Report*, p. 197, and *British Social Attitudes: The 1987 Report*, p. 225).

10 *How Britain Votes*, p. 135, and note, p. 140.

11 Gallup: the same question in 1979 produced a variation from 13 to 20 per cent; a differently worded question produced 20 per cent in 1983 and 23 per cent in 1987.

12 *British Social Attitudes: The 1986 Report*, p. 160.

13 *British Social Attitudes: The 1986 Report*, p. 172.

14 *The Gallup Survey of Britain*, p. 262

11 A Collective Future

1 It is impossible to estimate accurately what the 'natural' level of support for the parties would be, but Heath, Jowell and Curtice take the 1964 election as their starting point. It was a fairly average election for the 1959–70 period. If the various social groups had voted as they did in 1964, but taking into account the changes in class sizes (and the additional effects of changes in trade union membership and

housing tenure), by the mid-1980s the Tory vote would have increased to 47–50 per cent and the centre-party vote to about 13 per cent, while the Labour vote would have shrunk to 35–39 per cent (Anthony Heath and Sarah K. McDonald, 'Social Change and the Future of the Left', *Political Quarterly*, October 1987; and *How Britain Votes*, p. 52).

2 Mrs Thatcher, ITN *News At Ten*, 18 February 1988: 'Under our regime business hasn't done too badly'; and: 'Don't forget this regime has more than doubled the amount spent on the health service.'

3 *British Social Attitudes: The 1987 Report*, p. 181.

4 *New Statesman*, 6 June 1986.

5 And centre party supporters tend to be closer to Labour supporters than they are to Conservatives on defence policy (*British Social Attitudes: The 1986 Report*, pp. 48–9).

6 Although this question doesn't divide the parties as sharply as others, Alliance supporters still tended to be closer to Conservatives than to Labour supporters.

7 *British Social Attitudes: The 1987 Report*, pp. 56–7, 228. The 1959 study cited is the Civic Culture Study, reported by G. A. Almond and S. Verba, *The Civic Culture: Political Attitudes and Democracy in Five Nations*, Princeton University Press, 1963. In the eleven years from 1972 to 1983 Gallup also recorded a rise from 14 to 22 per cent in the proportion of people saying they thought 'people like yourself can, in a general way, influence changes in things that are not going well in the country' (Gallup Political Index, October 1972 and August 1983). The rise in the proportion saying they could influence changes between 1972 and 1983 occurred at the expense of 'Don't knows', which fell from 9 to 2 per cent; the proportion saying 'No, I can't influence changes' only fell from 77 to 75 per cent. This may seem to suggest that fatalism and cynicism are still the dominant moods, but the Social Attitudes survey shows that people are more assertive than the Gallup poll implies. And the level of satisfaction with the amount of influence they had didn't change much over much of this period – people may have thought they had more influence, but they still didn't think they had enough. When Gallup asked: 'In your opinion, do people like yourself have *enough* say in the way the government runs the country?' (my emphasis), in February 1973, 23 per cent said 'Yes', and in May 1978 only 20 per cent did.

8 Fabian Society pamphlet, an extract from which was published as 'From Here to Equality' in *The Guardian*, 2 May 1988.

Bibliography

M. Abrams, D. Gerard and N. Timms (eds), *Values and Social Change in Britain*, Macmillan, London, 1985.

Samuel Beer, *Britain Against Itself: The Political Contradictions of Collectivism*, Faber, London, (1982), 1983.

Daniel Bell, *The Cultural Contradictions of Capitalism*, Heinemann, Oxford, 1979.

British Election Studies: 1979 see Bo Särlvik; 1983 see Anthony Heath.

British Social Attitudes: survey findings referred to in this book cite the year of the survey, published a year later. Thus the 1983 findings are published in *British Social Attitudes: The 1984 Report*. *The 1984 Report* was edited by Roger Jowell and Colin Airey; *The 1985 Report* by Roger Jowell and Sharon Witherspoon; *The 1986 Report* and *The 1987 Report* by Roger Jowell, Sharon Witherspoon and Lindsay Brook; all published by Gower, Aldershot, for Social and Community Planning Research. Data from the 1987 survey (published as *The 5th* Report) was kindly supplied to me by the SCPR in advance of publication.

James Buchanan and Richard Wagner, *Democracy in Deficit: The Political Legacy of Lord Keynes*, Academic Press, New York, 1977.

Trevor Burridge, *Clement Attlee: A Political Biography*, Jonathan Cape, London, 1986.

David Butler and Trevor Kavanagh (eds), *The British General Election of 1987*, Macmillan, London, 1988.

Eric Deakins, *What Future for Labour?*, Hilary Shipman, London, 1988.

Decade of Dealignment, 1979 British Election Study: see Bo Särlvik.

Mark N. Franklin, *The Decline of Class Voting in Britain: Changes in the Basis of Electoral Choice, 1964–83*, Clarendon, Oxford, 1985.

Gallup surveys. Unless otherwise indicated, references to Gallup's findings are from Gallup Political Index, published monthly by Gallup in London. Many of Gallup's findings are collected in *The Gallup Report 1980* and *1981* (see Norman Webb) and in *The Gallup Survey of Britain*, published in 1986 (see Gordon Heald). Before 1975 many of them are collected in *The Gallup International Public Opinion Polls: Great Britain 1937–1975*, edited by George H. Gallup, Random House, New York, 1976.

Andrew Gamble, 'The Free Economy and the Strong State', in Ralph Miliband and John Saville (eds), *The Social Register 1979*, Merlin Press, London, 1979.

BIBLIOGRAPHY

John Goldthorpe, *Social Mobility and Class Structure in Modern Britain*, Clarendon Press, Oxford, 1980.

J. H. Goldthorpe, D. Lockwood, F. Bechhofer and J. Platt, *The Affluent Worker: Political Attitudes and Behaviour*, Cambridge University Press, 1968.

Bryan Gould, *Socialism and Freedom*, Macmillan, London, 1985.

David Graham and Peter Clarke, *The New Enlightenment: The Rebirth of Liberalism*, Macmillan, London, 1986.

S. Harding and D. Phillips, *Contrasting Values in Western Europe*, Macmillan, London, 1986.

Ralph Harris and Arthur Seldon, *Welfare Without the State: A Quarter-Century of Suppressed Public Choice*, Institute of Economic Affairs, 1987.

Roy Hattersley, *Choose Freedom*, Penguin, Harmondsworth, 1987.

Gordon Heald and Robert Wybrow, *The Gallup Survey of Britain*, Croom Helm, Beckenham, 1986.

Anthony Heath, Roger Jowell and John Curtice, *How Britain Votes* [based on 1983 British Election Study], Pergamon, Oxford, 1985.

Hilde T. Himmelweit, Patrick Humphreys, Marianne Jaeger and Michael Katz, *How Voters Decide*, Academic Press, London, 1981.

How Britain Votes, 1983 British Election Study: see Anthony Heath.

John MacInnes, *Thatcherism at Work*, Open University Press, Milton Keynes, 1987.

David Marquand, *The Unprincipled Society: New Demands and Old Politics*, Jonathan Cape, London, 1988.

Gordon Marshall, Howard Newby, David Rose and Carolyn Vogler, *Social Class in Modern Britain*, Hutchinson, London, 1988.

M. Rokeach, *The Nature of Human Values*, Free Press, New York, 1973.

Richard Rose, Mark Abrams and Rita Hinden, *Must Labour Lose?*, Penguin, Harmondsworth, 1960.

Bo Särlvik and Ivor Crewe, *Decade of Dealignment* [based on 1979 British Election Study], Cambridge University Press, 1983.

Adam Smith, *The Wealth of Nations*, edited by Andrew Skinner, 3rd edn, Penguin, Harmondsworth, 1979.

Norman Webb and Robert Wybrow, *The Gallup Report 1980*, Sphere, London, 1981.

Norman Webb and Robert Wybrow, *The Gallup Report 1981*, Sphere, London, 1982